FOOD&WINE

AMERICAN EXPRESS PUBLISHING CORPORATION, NEW YORK

FOOD & WINE COCKTAILS 2008

EDITOR **Kate Krader**
DEPUTY EDITOR **Jim Meehan**
SENIOR EDITOR **Colleen McKinney**
COPY EDITOR **Lisa Leventer**
RESEARCHERS **Janice Huang, Jennifer Salerno**
EDITORIAL ASSISTANT **Julia Bainbridge**

ART DIRECTOR **Patricia Sanchez**
DESIGNER **James Maikowski**
PRODUCTION MANAGER **Matt Carson**

PHOTOGRAPHY BY **Wendell T. Webber**
FOOD STYLING BY **Alison Attenborough**
PROP STYLING BY **Dani Fisher**

ON THE COVER El Gusano Rojo, p. 110

AMERICAN EXPRESS PUBLISHING CORPORATION

PRESIDENT/C.E.O. **Ed Kelly**
S.V.P./CHIEF MARKETING OFFICER **Mark V. Stanich**
C.F.O./S.V.P./CORPORATE DEVELOPMENT &
OPERATIONS **Paul B. Francis**
V.P., BOOKS & PRODUCTS **Marshall Corey**
SENIOR MARKETING MANAGER **Bruce Spanier**
ASSISTANT MARKETING MANAGER **Sarah Ross**
DIRECTOR OF FULFILLMENT **Phil Black**
MANAGER OF CUSTOMER EXPERIENCE &
PRODUCT DEVELOPMENT **Charles Graver**
BUSINESS MANAGER **Tom Noonan**
PRODUCTION DIRECTOR **Rosalie Abatemarco Samat**
CORPORATE PRODUCTION MANAGER
Stuart Handelman

ISBN 1-932624-25-2
ISSN 1554-4354

Published by American Express Publishing Corporation
1120 Avenue of the Americas, New York, NY 10036

Manufactured in the United States of America

*The names of companies and products mentioned in
this book may be the trademarks of their respective
owners. Reference to such third-party companies
and/or products is for informational purposes only
and is not intended to indicate or imply any affiliation,
association, sponsorship or endorsement.*

FOOD & WINE MAGAZINE

VICE PRESIDENT/EDITOR IN CHIEF **Dana Cowin**
CREATIVE DIRECTOR **Stephen Scoble**
MANAGING EDITOR **Mary Ellen Ward**
EXECUTIVE EDITOR **Pamela Kaufman**
EXECUTIVE FOOD EDITOR **Tina Ujlaki**
EXECUTIVE WINE EDITOR **Lettie Teague**

FEATURES
FEATURES EDITOR **Michelle Shih**
TRAVEL EDITOR **Salma Abdelnour**
SENIOR EDITORS **Ray Isle, Kate Krader**
ASSOCIATE EDITOR **Jen Murphy**
ASSISTANT EDITOR **Ratha Tep**
ASSISTANT HOME & STYLE EDITOR **Jessica Romm**
EDITORIAL ASSISTANTS **Alessandra Bulow,
Megan Krigbaum**

FOOD
SENIOR EDITOR **Kate Heddings**
SENIOR ASSOCIATE EDITOR **Nick Fauchald**
ASSOCIATE EDITOR **Emily Kaiser**
EDITORIAL ASSISTANT **Kristin Donnelly**
TEST KITCHEN SUPERVISOR **Marcia Kiesel**
SENIOR TEST KITCHEN ASSOCIATE **Grace Parisi**
TEST KITCHEN ASSOCIATE **Melissa Rubel**
KITCHEN ASSISTANT **Chris Fletcher**

ART
ART DIRECTOR **Patricia Sanchez**
SENIOR DESIGNER **Courtney Waddell**
DESIGNER **Michael Patti**
DESIGNER (BOOKS) **James Maikowski**

PHOTO
DIRECTOR OF PHOTOGRAPHY **Fredrika Stjärne**
ASSISTANT PHOTO EDITOR **Nicole Schilit**
PHOTO ASSISTANT **Rebecca Jacobs**

PRODUCTION
ASSISTANT MANAGING EDITOR **Christine Quinlan**
PRODUCTION MANAGER **Matt Carson**
DESIGN/PRODUCTION ASSISTANT **Carl Hesler**

COPY & RESEARCH
COPY CHIEF **Michele Berkover Petry**
SENIOR COPY EDITOR **Ann Lien**
ASSISTANT RESEARCH EDITORS **Emily McKenna,
Kelly Snowden, Emery Van Hook**

EDITORIAL BUSINESS COORDINATOR **Kerianne Hansen**

Cocktails 2008

FOOD&**WINE**
BOOKS

contents

foreword

To find the best cocktails, we sample hundreds of drinks from restaurants and bars across the country in the FOOD & WINE Test Kitchen. Not only do we have great fun, we also gain insight into the latest trends (2006—garnish overdrive; 2007—Manhattan mania). This year we've seen a proliferation of unusual ingredients in drinks, like miso paste; we've also noted a greater emphasis on true classic drinks, which is why we've devoted a whole chapter to them. In this edition, we've expanded our drinks lexicon with definitions of more than 50 spirits and mixers and added a listing of the top liquor stores nationwide. Lastly, we've included even more delicious bar-food recipes, because if there's anything a great cocktail needs, it's a bacon-wrapped, salsa-slathered hot dog to go with it.

DANA COWIN
EDITOR IN CHIEF
FOOD & WINE MAGAZINE

KATE KRADER
EDITOR
FOOD & WINE COCKTAILS 2008

cocktail clinic

bar tools

BOSTON SHAKER

The bartender's choice, consisting of a pint glass with a metal canister that covers the top to create a seal. Measure ingredients into the glass and shake with the metal half pointing away from you. Strain the drink from the canister.

COBBLER SHAKER

The most commonly used shaker, with a metal cup for mixing drinks with ice, a built-in strainer and a fitted top. There are generally two sizes of cobbler shakers: large, for multiple drinks, and individual, for single servings.

CITRUS JUICER

A shallow dish with a reaming cone, a spout and often a strainer that's used to separate juice from pulp. Juices are best the day they're squeezed, but orange and grapefruit juices can be refrigerated overnight.

MUDDLER

A sturdy, traditionally wooden tool that's used to crush herbs, sugar cubes and fresh fruit. Choose a muddler long enough to reach the bottom of your cocktail shaker; in a pinch, you can use a long-handled wooden spoon.

JIGGER

A two-sided stainless steel measuring instrument, indispensable for quick, precise mixing. Look for one with ½- and 1-ounce cups. A shot glass with measurements works well, too.

BAR SPOON

A long-handled metal spoon mixes and chills cocktails without creating cloudy air bubbles in spirits-only drinks like martinis, which look best when they're crystal clear. Bar spoons are also useful for measuring small amounts of liquid.

CHANNEL KNIFE

A small spoon-shaped knife with a metal tooth used for peeling long, thin fancy spiral twists from citrus fruit for garnish. A sharp paring knife or vegetable peeler works best for the wider citrus twists that are flamed (p. 16).

WAITER'S CORKSCREW

A pocketknife-like tool with a bottle opener and a small blade used for cutting foil from wine caps. Bartenders prefer this model to the bulkier and more complicated corkscrews available.

HAWTHORNE STRAINER

The best all-purpose strainer. This round metal device has a semicircular spring that ensures a snug, spill-proof fit on top of a shaker. Look for a tightly coiled spring, which will keep muddled fruit and herbs out of your drink.

JULEP STRAINER

The preferred device for straining cocktails from a pint glass. Fine holes keep ice out of the finished cocktail, and the shape fits securely inside a mixing glass. If you don't have a julep strainer, a Hawthorne strainer will do the trick.

glassware arsenal

1. RED WINE

A balloon-shaped glass for fruity cocktails as well as punches. Stemless versions are fine stand-ins for snifters.

2. MARTINI

A stemmed glass with a cone-shaped bowl for cocktails that are served straight up (chilled with ice, then strained).

3. HIGHBALL

A tall, narrow glass that helps preserve the fizz in drinks served on ice and topped with soda or tonic water.

4. ROCKS

A short, sturdy, wide-mouthed glass for spirits served neat and cocktails poured over ice.

5. FLUTE

A tall, slender glass whose shape helps keep Champagne and sparkling-wine cocktails effervescent.

6. SNIFTER

A wide-bowled glass, designed to rest in your palm, for warm drinks, cocktails served on ice and spirits served neat.

7. CORDIAL

A petite, tulip-shaped glass for powerful drinks served in very small portions, dessert wines and liqueurs served neat.

8. PINT

A tall, flared glass with a wide mouth used for stirring or shaking, and serving oversize drinks.

9. COUPE

A shallow, wide-mouthed glass primarily used for small (a.k.a. short), potent cocktails.

10. WHITE WINE

A tall, narrow glass for wine-based cocktails. A fine substitute for a highball glass.

11. PILSNER

A thin, flared glass useful for beer as well as cocktails too large for a highball; can also accommodate multiple garnishes.

12. COLLINS

A taller, narrower glass than a highball commonly used for drinks served on ice and topped with a large amount of soda.

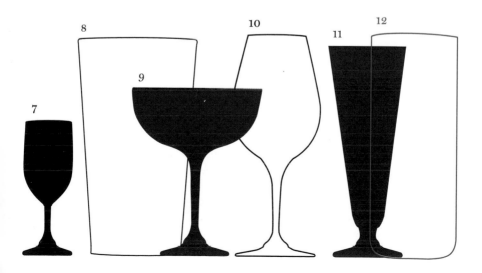

cocktail clinic

cocktail basics

simple syrup

This bar staple is one of the most universal mixers, essential to many well-balanced cocktails. Stash a jar in your refrigerator; it keeps for up to 1 month.

MAKES ABOUT 12 OUNCES
Combine 1 cup water and 1 cup sugar in a small saucepan and bring to a boil over moderately high heat, stirring to dissolve the sugar, about 3 minutes. Remove from the heat and let cool. Refrigerate in a tightly covered glass jar until ready to use.

grenadine

This lightly tart pomegranate-flavored mixer adds color and sweetness to drinks. For a tarter syrup, simply decrease the amount of sugar here by half.

MAKES ABOUT 16 OUNCES
In a medium saucepan, simmer 16 ounces unsweetened pomegranate juice with 1 cup plus 2 tablespoons sugar over moderate heat until thick enough to coat the back of a spoon, about 15 minutes. Add ⅛ teaspoon orange flower water. Refrigerate in an airtight container for up to 2 weeks.

"ginger beer"

This uncarbonated staple was adapted from Dale DeGroff's *Craft of the Cocktail*. Although it's a syrup, pros refer to it as "ginger beer." To make your own fizzy version, stir together equal parts of the syrup and ginger ale.

MAKES ABOUT 32 OUNCES
In a medium saucepan, bring 4 cups water to a boil. Remove from the heat and add ⅔ cup finely chopped fresh ginger, ¾ ounce fresh lime juice and 5 tablespoons light brown sugar. Let steep for 1 hour, stirring occasionally. Pour the syrup through a fine strainer, pressing on the solids. Refrigerate in an airtight container for up to 3 days.

CONVERSION CHART

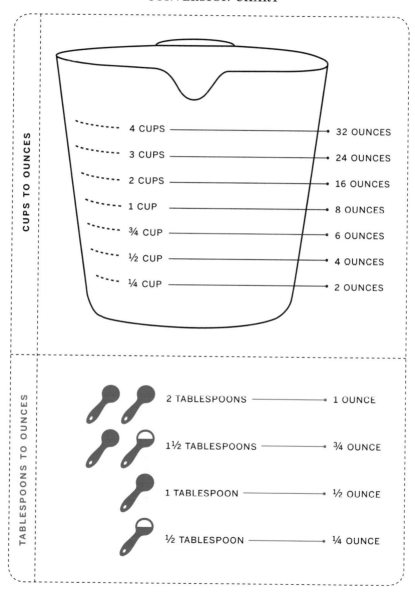

CUPS TO OUNCES

4 CUPS	32 OUNCES
3 CUPS	24 OUNCES
2 CUPS	16 OUNCES
1 CUP	8 OUNCES
¾ CUP	6 OUNCES
½ CUP	4 OUNCES
¼ CUP	2 OUNCES

TABLESPOONS TO OUNCES

2 TABLESPOONS	1 OUNCE
1½ TABLESPOONS	¾ OUNCE
1 TABLESPOON	½ OUNCE
½ TABLESPOON	¼ OUNCE

cocktail basics

RIMMING A GLASS

To coat the rim of a glass, place a few spoonfuls of salt (preferably kosher), sugar (preferably superfine) or other powdered or finely crushed ingredient on a small plate. Moisten the outer rim of the glass with a citrus fruit wedge, water or a colorful liquid like pomegranate juice, then roll it on the plate until lightly coated. Hold the glass upside down and tap to release any excess. Bartenders often coat only half of the rim so there's a choice of sides to sip from.

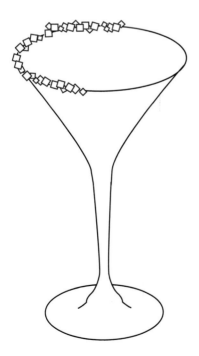

MAKING A TWIST

A twist adds concentrated citrus flavor from the peel's essential oils. To make a twist, cut a quarter-size disk of the peel, avoiding the white pith. Gently grasp the outer edges of the disk skin side down between the thumb and two fingers and pinch the twist over the top of the drink. Rub the peel around the rim of the glass, then drop it into the drink.

FLAMING A TWIST

Flaming a lemon or orange twist caramelizes the zest's essential oils. First cut a thin, oval, quarter-size piece of zest with a bit of the white pith intact. Gently grasp the outer edges skin side down between the thumb and two fingers and hold the twist about 4 inches over the cocktail. Hold a lit match over the drink an inch away from the twist (don't let the flame touch the peel), then pinch the edges of the twist sharply so the citrus oil falls through the flame and into the drink.

DOUBLE SHAKING

Cocktails made with eggs should be shaken well to emulsify them. To accomplish this without over-diluting the drink, add all ingredients—except ice or carbonated beverages—to the shaker and shake for 10 seconds (known as "dry shaking"). Then add the ice and shake the drink again.

DOUBLE STRAINING

Drinks made with muddled fruit and herbs are sometimes double strained to remove tiny particles, so the cocktail is pristine and clear. To double strain, place a very fine tea strainer over the serving glass. Make the drink in a shaker, then set a Hawthorne strainer over the shaker and pour the drink through both strainers into the glass.

PERFECT ICE CUBES

Using the correct ice is key to a great drink. For most drinks, the bigger the ice, the better. Large pieces of ice melt more slowly, and dilute drinks less. Detail-obsessed bars such as Milk & Honey in New York City cut their ice from large blocks. The exception to the big ice rule: the crushed ice in juleps and swizzled drinks. Besides melting quickly, which dilutes potent drinks, crushed ice also adds an appealing frost to glasses.

To make crushed ice, cover cubes in a clean kitchen towel and pound with a hammer or rolling pin.

To make clear cubes, fill ice trays with hot filtered water.

For perfectly square cubes, use Tovolo's flexible silicone Perfect Cube ice trays (surlatable.com).

drinks lexicon

This glossary features many of the spirits, mixers and other ingredients in this book. They can be found at most liquor stores (see our list of the best nationwide on p. 218) and from online spirits retailers.

Absinthe An anise-flavored spirit banned in the United States in 1912 in part because its namesake ingredient, *Artemisia absinthium*, or wormwood, was thought to be toxic in large doses. Absinthe containing amounts of wormwood deemed acceptable is now available in the U.S.

Amaro A bittersweet Italian herbal liqueur often served as a digestif.

Angostura bitters A brand of concentrated aromatic bitters created in Angostura, Venezuela, in 1824 from a secret combination of herbs and spices.

Aperol A bitter orange Italian aperitif flavored with rhubarb and gentian.

Apfelkorn A low-proof apple schnapps made by blending a wheat-based spirit with sugar and fresh apples.

Apple brandy A distilled fermented apple cider that is aged in oak barrels and usually 80 to 90 proof in strength. Bonded apple brandy, which is preferable in cocktails because of its strong green-apple flavor, is 100 proof.

Aquavit A grain- or potato-based spirit flavored with caraway seeds and other botanicals, such as fennel, anise and citrus peel.

Bärenjäger An intensely honey-flavored proprietary German liqueur.

Batavia Arrack A clear spirit from Java that is made from fermented sugarcane and red rice.

Becherovka A bittersweet liqueur produced in the Czech Republic from the recipe that pharmacist Josef Becher used to formulate his apothecary bitters in 1807.

Belle de Brillet A French liqueur made by infusing Cognac with macerated ripe Alsatian pears.

Bénédictine A brandy-based herbal liqueur derived from a recipe that was developed by French monks in 1510.

Bianco vermouth An aromatic, sweet Italian white vermouth traditionally served on the rocks as an aperitif.

Bitters A superconcentrated solution of bitter and often aromatic plants that adds flavor and complexity to drinks. Varieties include orange, lemon, peach and aromatic bitters, the best known of which is Angostura.

Cachaça A potent Brazilian spirit distilled from fresh sugarcane juice; some of the best versions are made in copper pot stills and aged in wooden casks.

Calvados A cask-aged brandy made in France's Normandy region from apples and sometimes pears.

Campari A bright red bitter Italian aperitif made from herbs and fruit.

Carpano Antica Formula A rich and complex, crimson-colored sweet Italian vermouth.

Chartreuse A spicy French liqueur made from 130 herbs; green Chartreuse is more potent than the honey-sweetened yellow variety.

Cherry Heering A brandy-based Danish cherry liqueur.

Cointreau A distilled proprietary French triple sec that is flavored with the essential oils of sun-dried sweet and bitter orange peels.

Crème de cassis A sweet, black currant–flavored liqueur.

Crème de violette A sweet, violet-flavored and -colored liqueur.

Créole Shrubb A potent liqueur made by infusing a blend of Martinican rums with bitter orange peel and pulp and Caribbean spices.

Cynar A pleasantly bitter Italian liqueur made from 13 herbs and plants, including artichokes.

Dubonnet rouge A bittersweet red wine–based aperitif containing spices and quinine; the recipe dates to 1846.

Eau-de-vie A clear, unaged fruit brandy. Varieties include kirsch (cherry), framboise (raspberry), mirabelle (plum) and poire (pear).

Fernet-Branca A bitter Italian digestif made from 27 herbs.

Galliano A yellow Italian liqueur made with up to 30 herbs, berries and flowers, including licorice, anise and vanilla.

Grenadine A sweet syrup made from pomegranate juice and sugar (recipe, p. 14).

Herbsaint An anise-flavored absinthe substitute produced in New Orleans.

drinks lexicon

Kirsch Short for *kirschwasser;* an unaged brandy or eau-de-vie produced by pot-distilling crushed cherries and their pits.

Licor 43 An orange-and-vanilla-flavored Spanish liqueur made from a combination of 43 herbs and spices.

Lillet A wine-based French aperitif flavored with orange peel and quinine. The rare red (rouge) variety is sweeter than the more common white (blanc) variety.

Limoncello An intensely flavored Italian liqueur made from lemon peels soaked in neutral spirits, then sweetened with sugar.

Madeira A fortified wine from the island of Madeira, usually named for one of four grape varieties: **Sercial** (the driest), **Verdelho, Bual** or **Malmsey,** which are progressively sweeter.

Maraschino liqueur A clear Italian liqueur, the best of which is made from bittersweet marasca cherries, aged in ash barrels, then diluted and sweetened with sugar.

Mezcal An agave-based spirit with a smoky flavor that comes from roasting the agave hearts in pits before fermentation. The best mezcal is made in Mexico's Oaxaca region.

Navan A brandy infused with black Madagascar vanilla.

Nocino An Italian or Swiss liqueur traditionally made from brandy or grappa, unripe walnuts, sugar and spices.

Orgeat A lightly sweet, nonalcoholic, almond-flavored syrup that is accented with orange flower water.

Pastis A licorice-flavored French spirit that turns cloudy when mixed with water. It's similar to absinthe but sweeter and lower in alcohol.

Pernod A French pastis produced by extracting the essential oils from star anise and fennel, then combining them with a blend of herbs, spices, water, sugar and a neutral spirit.

Peychaud's bitters A brand of bitters with bright anise and cranberry flavors; the recipe dates to 18th-century New Orleans.

Pimm's No. 1 A gin-based English aperitif often served with citrus-flavored soda or ginger beer.

Pineau des Charentes A low-proof French spirit made by combining unfermented grape juice and young Cognac, then briefly aging in oak.

Pisco A clear spirit distilled from grapes in the wine-producing regions of Peru and Chile.

Pommeau de Normandie A French aperitif spirit made by adding fresh-pressed apple juice to young Calvados, then aging it in oak.

Port A fortified wine from the Douro region of Portugal. Styles include fruity, young **Ruby** ports; richer, nuttier **Tawnies; thick-textured, oak-aged **Late Bottled Vintage (LBV)** versions; and decadent **Vintage** ports, made from the best grapes in the best vintages.

Punt e Mes A spicy, orange-accented sweet vermouth fortified with bitters.

Rhum agricole An aromatic rum made in the French West Indies from sugarcane juice. When aged from one to six months, it is bottled as white *rhum agricole,* or *rhum blanc;* aged for a minimum of three years, it can be sold as aged *rhum agricole,* or *rhum vieux.*

Rye whiskey A primarily rye-based distilled spirit, often blended with corn mash and barley. American straight rye whiskey is produced from a mash of at least 51 percent rye, aged in new charred oak barrels for at least two years and diluted with nothing but water.

Sherry A fortified wine from Spain's Jerez region. Varieties include dry, fresh styles like **Manzanilla;** nuttier, richer **Amontillados** and **Palo Cortados;** and viscous sweet versions such as **cream sherry** and **Pedro Ximénez.**

Sloe gin A bittersweet red liqueur with a nutty finish made by infusing a neutral grain spirit or gin with sloe berries and sugar.

Strega An Italian liqueur infused with more than 70 herbs and spices, including saffron, which gives it a golden yellow color.

Triple sec An orange-flavored distilled neutral spirit. **Cointreau** is the premium proprietary triple sec, created in France in 1875.

Velvet Falernum A low-alcohol, sugarcane-based liqueur from Barbados flavored with clove, almond and lime.

Vermouth An aromatic fortified wine. It can be white or red, and ranges from dry (used in martinis) to very sweet (often served as an aperitif).

MANHATTAN, P. 28
"Pulse" coupes by Calvin Klein.

classics

negroni

This cocktail probably got its name from Camillo Negroni, a Florentine aristocrat who liked his Americano (sweet vermouth, Campari and soda) with a splash of gin.

Ice
1 ounce gin
1 ounce sweet vermouth
1 ounce Campari
1 orange twist

Fill a pint glass with ice. Add the gin, vermouth and Campari and stir well. Strain into a chilled coupe and garnish with the orange twist.

martini

This recipe is adapted from the version in George Kappeler's 1895 *Modern American Drinks*. It was originally made with Old Tom gin, a sweetened gin unlike the London dry gin in the present-day martini.

Ice
3 ounces gin
1 ounce dry vermouth
2 dashes of orange bitters
1 lemon twist or 1 green olive

Fill a pint glass with ice. Add the gin, vermouth and bitters and stir well. Strain into a chilled martini glass or coupe and garnish with the lemon twist or olive.

MARTINI
*"Aarne" cocktail glasses by
iittala; tray by Mepra.*

PISCO SOUR
*"Paolo C." coupe from
Takashimaya; "Drops"
vase by Salviati.*

pisco sour

The national cocktail of Chile and Peru, this drink may have evolved from the Pisco Punch, which was all the rage in San Francisco during the 1849 gold rush.

2 ounces pisco
¾ ounce fresh lemon juice
¾ ounce Simple Syrup (p. 14)
1 large egg white
Ice
4 drops of Angostura bitters

Put all of the ingredients except the ice and bitters in a cocktail shaker; shake for 10 seconds. Add ice; shake for 10 more seconds, then strain into a chilled coupe. Dot the drink with the bitters and draw a straw through the drops.

margarita

Arguably the most popular cocktail today in the United States, the margarita is said to have been invented in the 1930s by the manager of the Garci Crespo Hotel in Puebla, Mexico, whose girlfriend, Margarita, loved salt with whatever she happened to be drinking.

2 lime wedges and kosher salt
Ice
2 ounces blanco tequila
¾ ounce Cointreau or other triple sec
¾ ounce fresh lime juice
¼ ounce Simple Syrup (p. 14)

Moisten half of the outer rim of a coupe with 1 of the lime wedges and coat lightly with salt. Fill a cocktail shaker with ice, add all of the remaining ingredients and shake well. Strain into the prepared coupe and garnish with the remaining lime wedge.

classics

manhattan

According to popular legend, this cocktail was created at the Manhattan Club in 1874, at a party given by Winston Churchill's American mother to celebrate Samuel J. Tilden's election as governor of New York.

Ice
2 ounces rye whiskey
1 ounce sweet vermouth
2 dashes of Angostura bitters
3 maraschino cherries
  skewered on a pick

Fill a pint glass with ice. Add the rye, vermouth and bitters and stir well. Strain into a chilled coupe and garnish with the skewered cherries.

sazerac

New Orleans's famous Sazerac cocktail can be traced back to the 1850s, when it was made at the Sazerac Coffee House using Sazerac-de-Forge et Fils Cognac and bitters produced at Antoine Peychaud's apothecary just a few blocks away.

¼ ounce absinthe or Pernod
1 sugar cube
2 dashes of Angostura bitters
3 dashes of Peychaud's bitters
Ice
2 ounces rye whiskey
1 lemon twist

Rinse a chilled rocks glass with the absinthe, then pour it out. In a pint glass, muddle the sugar cube with the Angostura and Peychaud's bitters. Add ice and the rye and stir well to chill the drink and dissolve the sugar. Strain into the prepared rocks glass. Pinch the lemon twist over the drink, rub it around the rim and discard.

champagne cocktail

According to cocktail historian David Wondrich, this drink was so popular in the late 1800s that celebrated bartender Jerry Thomas ordered 100 cases of Champagne at a time to keep his bar stocked.

5 ounces chilled Champagne
2 dashes of Angostura bitters
1 sugar cube
1 lemon twist

Pour the Champagne into a chilled flute. Sprinkle the bitters on the sugar cube and add it to the flute. Garnish with the lemon twist.

old-fashioned

"Whiskey Old-Fashioned" actually refers to two cocktails. One consists of whiskey, sugar, bitters, ice and a lemon peel. The better-known, fancier version of the drink, made with muddled orange and a cherry, is listed as "Old Fashioned No. 2" in the 1934 edition of *"Cocktail Bill" Boothby's World Drinks and How to Mix Them.*

2 orange wheels, 1 skewered on a pick with 1 brandied cherry
3 brandied cherries
½ ounce Simple Syrup (p. 14)
3 dashes of Angostura bitters
Ice
2 ounces bourbon
1 ounce chilled club soda

In a cocktail shaker, muddle the orange wheel with the 3 cherries, the Simple Syrup and the bitters. Add ice and the bourbon and shake well. Strain into an ice-filled rocks glass. Stir in the club soda and garnish with the skewered orange wheel and cherry.

mojito

Made with fresh lime, muddled mint, sugar and rum, the mojitos at La Bodeguita del Medio in Havana were immortalized by Ernest Hemingway, the most celebrated 20th-century barfly.

8 mint leaves, plus 1 mint sprig
1 ounce Simple Syrup (p. 14)
¾ ounce fresh lime juice
Ice
2 ounces white rum
1 ounce chilled club soda

In a cocktail shaker, muddle the mint leaves with the Simple Syrup and lime juice. Add ice and the rum and shake well. Strain into an ice-filled highball glass. Stir in the club soda and garnish with the mint sprig.

dark 'n stormy

According to a Gosling's Rum tale, this drink was invented more than 100 years ago when members of Bermuda's Royal Naval Officer's Club added a splash of the local rum to their spicy homemade ginger beer. They described its ominous hue as "the color of a cloud only a fool or dead man would sail under."

Ice
2 ounces dark rum, preferably Gosling's
½ ounce fresh lime juice (optional)
3 ounces chilled ginger beer
1 candied ginger slice skewered on a pick with 1 lime wheel

Fill a cocktail shaker with ice. Add the rum and lime juice and shake well. Strain into an ice-filled collins glass. Stir in the ginger beer and garnish with the skewered candied ginger and lime wheel.

DARK 'N STORMY
*"Random Cut" glass
by Calvin Klein.*

HEIGHTS COBBLER, P. 44
JACK THE HORSE TAVERN,
BROOKLYN, NY
*Old-fashioned glass by Kikatsu
from Eastern Accent.*

wine, beer & aperitifs

commodore perry

PDT,
MANHATTAN

This version of pioneering mixologist Jerry Thomas's classic Japanese Cocktail takes its name from Matthew C. Perry, an American naval officer whose Pacific voyages in the 1850s helped secure U.S. trade relations with Japan.

Ice
1 ounce Cognac
½ ounce pineapple juice
½ ounce orgeat (almond-flavored syrup)
2 ounces chilled Champagne

Fill a cocktail shaker with ice. Add the Cognac, pineapple juice and orgeat and shake well. Strain into a chilled coupe and top with the Champagne.

summer rye

TAO BEACH,
LAS VEGAS

At Tao Beach, the rooftop pool bar at the Venetian Hotel, the bartenders use only fresh-squeezed fruit juices for drinks such as this effervescent cocktail.

Ice
1½ ounces rye whiskey
¾ ounce elderflower liqueur
1 ounce apple juice
¾ ounce fresh lemon juice
¾ ounce chilled Champagne
1 thin apple slice

Fill a cocktail shaker with ice. Add the rye, elderflower liqueur and apple and lemon juices; shake well. Strain into a chilled coupe, top with the Champagne and garnish with the apple slice.

belle de jour

EASTERN STANDARD,
BOSTON

Like many top cocktail bars, Eastern Standard makes its own syrups, including the grenadine that gives Belle de Jour its blushing color and hint of bittersweet pomegranate.

Ice
½ ounce Bénédictine (brandy-based herbal liqueur)
½ ounce Cognac
½ ounce grenadine, preferably homemade (p. 14)
½ ounce fresh lemon juice
3 ounces chilled Champagne
1 lemon twist

Fill a cocktail shaker with ice. Add the Bénédictine, Cognac, grenadine and lemon juice and shake well. Strain into a chilled flute and top with the Champagne. Garnish with the lemon twist.

angel

THE BEEHIVE,
BOSTON

Named after a 1920s Paris artists' collective called La Ruche (The Beehive), this self-proclaimed "neighborhood *café des artistes*" incorporates French spirits in nearly all of its Champagne cocktails.

Ice
¼ ounce Chambord
1 ounce Pineau des Charentes (Cognac-fortified grape juice) or Lillet blanc
4 ounces chilled Champagne

Fill a pint glass with ice. Add the Chambord and Pineau des Charentes and stir well. Strain into a chilled flute and top the drink with the Champagne.

mirabelle

GEORGE'S AT THE COVE, SAN DIEGO

Chef Trey Foshee prefers using mirabelle plums from the renowned Chino Farms in nearby Rancho Santa Fe for his restaurant's unusual Champagne cocktail.

Ice
¾ ounce Plum Puree (below)
¼ ounce Pernod
4½ ounces chilled Champagne
2 red plum slices

Fill a pint glass with ice. Add the Plum Puree, Pernod and Champagne and stir gently. Strain into a chilled flute and garnish with the plum slices.

PLUM PUREE In a small saucepan, bring 8 ounces water to a boil with ½ cup sugar and 3 ounces fresh lemon juice. Add 3 quartered pitted plums and simmer over moderate heat until the plums begin to fall apart, about 30 minutes. Let cool, then puree in a blender and strain into a bowl. Refrigerate, covered, for up to 3 days. Makes about 8 ounces.

MIRABELLE

*"Jean" flute by Marc
Jacobs for Waterford;
vintage glass candy dish
from The End of History.*

la rosa

FLATIRON LOUNGE,
MANHATTAN

Flatiron Lounge co-owner Julie Reiner thought up this drink during a cruise last year after her first taste of orange-spiced Ramazzotti *amaro* in Sicily.

2 strawberry slices
½ ounce Simple Syrup (p. 14)
Ice
2 ounces blanco tequila
1 ounce *amaro* (bittersweet Italian liqueur)
¾ ounce fresh lemon juice
1½ ounces chilled rosé Champagne
1 edible pansy (optional)

In a cocktail shaker, muddle the strawberry slices with the Simple Syrup. Add ice and the tequila, *amaro* and lemon juice and shake well. Strain into a white wine glass, top with the Champagne and garnish with the pansy.

the fall bride

THE GREAT NABOB,
SEATTLE

In early 2007, a bride-to-be asked Great Nabob owner Devlin McGill to create a drink for her autumn wedding that would taste like chocolate-dipped berries but not like candy. This cocktail is the result.

Ice
1 ounce raspberry vodka
½ ounce coffee liqueur
½ ounce Simple Syrup (p. 14)
3 ounces chilled Prosecco
1 raspberry

In a pint glass, stir everything but the Prosecco and raspberry. Strain into a chilled flute and top with the Prosecco. Garnish with the raspberry.

blanc de fraise

CIRCA,
HIGH BRIDGE, NJ

This cocktail's name is a play on Champagne terminology. Blanc de Noirs refers to Champagne made with 100 percent Pinot Noir grapes; Blanc de Blancs are Champagnes made with only Chardonnay. Cava, a Spanish sparkling wine made from a blend of grapes, has a light, refreshing quality that works well with strawberries, or *fraises.*

3   strawberries, diced,
plus 1 strawberry slice
½   ounce Simple Syrup (p. 14)
Ice
1   ounce gin
¾   ounce Cointreau or other triple sec
2½   ounces chilled cava

In a cocktail shaker, muddle the diced strawberries with the Simple Syrup. Add ice and the gin and Cointreau and shake well. Strain into a chilled martini glass. Top with the cava and garnish with the strawberry slice.

sgroppino

TEMPLE BAR,
MANHATTAN

During a solo trip to Italy, Kiki Kogelnik called her husband, Temple Bar owner George Schwarz, to say she'd just tasted the drink of her life, the Sgroppino. To welcome his wife home, Schwarz added the drink to his menu.

½   ounce citrus vodka
2   small scoops of lemon sorbet
¼   ounce fresh lemon juice
3   ounces chilled Prosecco

In a pint glass, combine the vodka, sorbet and lemon juice and stir well. Add the Prosecco, stir again and pour into a chilled flute.

grapefruit flamingo

SOLSTICE,
SAN FRANCISCO

This sparkling, rose-colored cocktail in a long-stemmed flute reminded creator Kieran Walsh of the long-legged tropical bird.

Ice

- 1 ounce Grapefruit Vodka (below)
- ¼ ounce Campari
- 4 ounces chilled sparkling wine
- 1 grapefruit twist

Fill a pint glass with ice. Add the Grapefruit Vodka and Campari and stir well. Strain into a chilled flute. Top with the sparkling wine and garnish with the grapefruit twist.

GRAPEFRUIT VODKA In a jar, combine 8 ounces vodka with the finely grated zest of 1 pink grapefruit and let stand for 2 hours. Strain into an airtight container and refrigerate for up to 1 month. Makes 8 ounces.

pecan ratafia

**T'AFIA,
HOUSTON**

T'afia makes its ratafias by soaking seasonal fruits, vegetables or herbs in wine and a spirit for anywhere from two weeks to a month. This unusual pecan-flavored drink is one of more than 100 ratafias served here, although only a few are on the menu at any given time.

MAKES 8 DRINKS

- 1 cup toasted pecans, chopped
- ¼ cup sugar
- ¼ vanilla bean, seeds scraped
- 2 ounces vodka
- 1 bottle (750 ml) crisp white wine

Ice

In an airtight container, combine the pecans, sugar, vanilla bean, vodka and wine and refrigerate for 1 week, stirring occasionally. Strain the drink into ice-filled rocks glasses.

chrysanthemum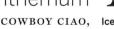

**COWBOY CIAO,
SCOTTSDALE, AZ**

A version of this drink appears in the 1930 *Savoy Cocktail Book* by Harry Craddock. He noted that it was "very popular in the American Bar of the S.S. *Europa*," one of the great transatlantic liners that carried cocktail-deprived Americans to Europe during Prohibition.

Ice

- 2 ounces dry vermouth
- 1 ounce Bénédictine (brandy-based herbal liqueur)
- 3 dashes of absinthe or Pernod
- 1 orange twist

Fill a pint glass with ice. Add the vermouth, Bénédictine and absinthe and stir well. Strain into a chilled coupe and garnish with the orange twist.

GREEN WITH ENVY
*"Fern" Champagne saucer
by William Yeoward.*

pimm's cup

NAPOLEON HOUSE,
NEW ORLEANS

The Pimm's Cup, a great refresher in New Orleans's sultry climate, is the drink of choice at the Napoleon House, a 19th-century tavern owned by the Impastato family.

Ice
1½ ounces Pimm's No. 1 (English gin-based aperitif)
2½ ounces fresh lemon juice
1 ounce Simple Syrup (p. 14)
1½ ounces chilled 7-Up
1 unpeeled cucumber wheel

Fill a cocktail shaker with ice. Add the Pimm's, lemon juice and Simple Syrup and shake well. Strain into an ice-filled collins glass. Stir in the 7-Up and garnish with the cucumber wheel.

green with envy

POLENG LOUNGE,
SAN FRANCISCO

Tea is an ingredient in almost all of the specialty drinks and many of the Asian-street-food-inspired dishes at this restaurant and lounge.

½ large green apple, seeded and chopped, plus 1 apple slice
¼ ounce Simple Syrup (p. 14)
Ice
3 ounces chilled sake
2 ounces chilled brewed green tea

In a pint glass, muddle the chopped apple with the Simple Syrup. Add ice and the sake and green tea and stir well. Double strain (p. 17) into a chilled coupe and garnish with the apple slice.

heights cobbler

JACK THE HORSE TAVERN,
BROOKLYN, NY

Location inspired the fruity ingredients in this drink. The Brooklyn Heights tavern is on Cranberry Street, one block from Orange Street and two blocks from Pineapple Street.

½ lemon wheel and ½ orange wheel
6 fresh or thawed frozen cranberries
2 pineapple spears, 1 peeled
Ice
2 ounces Ruby port
½ ounce Grand Marnier
2 dashes of aromatic bitters, preferably Fee's

In a cocktail shaker, muddle the lemon and orange wheels with 3 cranberries and the peeled pineapple. Add ice and the port, Grand Marnier and bitters and shake well. Strain into an ice-filled rocks glass; garnish with 3 cranberries and the unpeeled pineapple spear.

amberjack

LE COLONIAL,
SAN FRANCISCO

Mixing beer like the apple lambic here into a cocktail may sound like a new trick, but old cocktail books are filled with beer concoctions. Lambics are Belgian beers that are fermented with wild yeasts.

Ice
1 ounce apple vodka
½ ounce Macallan Amber (Scotch-based maple-flavored liqueur)
½ ounce Calvados
½ ounce fresh lime juice
1½ ounces chilled apple lambic
1 thin green apple slice

Fill a cocktail shaker with ice. Add the vodka, Macallan Amber, Calvados and lime juice; shake well. Strain into a chilled martini glass, stir in the lambic and garnish with the apple slice.

bergamot shandy

This Cal-Med restaurant, named for its "north of the Panhandle" neighborhood moniker, occupies a former bank. The vault is a constant and cool 56 degrees, perfect for storing spirits and wines.

Ice

- ¾ ounce *amaro* (bittersweet Italian liqueur)
- ¾ ounce Créole Shrubb or Grand Marnier
- 3 drops of orange flower water
- 5 ounces chilled lager
- 1 ounce chilled ginger beer
- ¼ teaspoon finely grated orange zest

Fill a pint glass with ice. Add the *amaro*, Créole Shrubb and orange flower water and stir well. Strain into a chilled pilsner glass and stir in the lager and ginger beer. Garnish with the grated orange zest.

GREEN TEA-NI, P. 57
JADE BAR,
PARADISE VALLEY, AZ
*"Twigs" martini glass
by Johanna Grawunder
for Salviati.*

vodka

basil 8

TABLE 8,
MIAMI BEACH

Consulting mixologist Ryan Magarian's combination of grape, lime and basil complements the savory flavors in chef Govind Armstrong's coastal American dishes at the Miami location of Armstrong's Los Angeles restaurant.

6 Thai basil leaves
6 Concord grapes
1 ounce Simple Syrup (p. 14)
Ice
1½ ounces vodka
¾ ounce fresh lime juice
Dash of Angostura bitters
1 ounce chilled ginger ale

In a cocktail shaker, muddle 4 of the basil leaves with 4 of the grapes and the Simple Syrup. Add ice and the vodka, lime juice and bitters and shake well. Strain into an ice-filled collins glass and stir in the ginger ale. Garnish with the remaining 2 basil leaves and 2 grapes.

mint lemonade

IKE'S COFFEE BAR
& COCKTAILS,
TUCSON

Cocktails made with honey often include the word "bee," as in Bee's Kiss or Bee's Knees, but this drink's sweet sting is a surprise.

Ice
1½ ounces vodka
1½ ounces fresh lemon juice
¾ ounce Honey Syrup (below)
½ ounce Simple Syrup (p. 14)
1 mint sprig

Fill a cocktail shaker with ice. Add the vodka, lemon juice, Honey Syrup and Simple Syrup and shake well. Strain into an ice-filled highball glass and garnish with the mint sprig.

HONEY SYRUP In a small saucepan, melt ½ cup honey in 4 ounces water over moderate heat until blended. Remove from the heat and let cool, then refrigerate in an airtight container for up to 2 weeks. Makes about 6 ounces.

vodka

napa valley fizz

FLEUR DE LYS,
LAS VEGAS

Like the flagship Fleur de Lys in San Francisco, the newer Vegas outpost uses nonalcoholic Gewürztraminer grape juice from Navarro Vineyards in Mendocino County, California, for this cooling fizz.

Ice
1½ ounces vodka
1 ounce white grape juice
½ ounce fresh lemon juice
¼ ounce Simple Syrup (p. 14)
1 ounce chilled club soda
½ ounce crème de cassis (black-currant liqueur)
1 small bunch of seedless green grapes

Fill a cocktail shaker with ice. Add the vodka, white grape juice, lemon juice and Simple Syrup and shake well. Strain into an ice-filled white wine glass. Stir in the chilled club soda and pour the crème de cassis on top; it will sink to the bottom. Garnish with the grapes.

NAPA VALLEY FIZZ
*"Eva" goblet by Eva Zeisel
for Nambé.*

sonoma fog vinotini

FLEMING'S PRIME
STEAKHOUSE & WINE BAR,
MADISON, WI

The ingenious frothy ice wine topping on this drink looks like the fog that creeps over Sonoma in the evening.

Ice
1½ ounces vodka
¾ ounce Cointreau or other triple sec
½ ounce fresh lemon juice
½ ounce Simple Syrup (p. 14)
Ice Wine–Lime Froth (below)
1-inch-wide wedge of pink grapefruit

Fill a cocktail shaker with ice. Add the vodka, Cointreau, lemon juice and Simple Syrup and shake well. Strain into a chilled martini glass. Carefully top with the Ice Wine–Lime Froth and garnish with the grapefruit wedge.

ICE WINE–LIME FROTH In a cocktail shaker, combine 1 large egg white, ½ ounce fresh lime juice, ½ ounce ice wine and ¼ ounce Cointreau or other triple sec and shake for 10 seconds. Add ice and shake for 10 more seconds. Scoop out the froth, discarding the ice cubes, and use immediately. Makes enough froth for 1 drink.

au provence

MUZE LOUNGE,
SCOTTSDALE, AZ

The savory flavor of this fresh lime gimlet (a drink traditionally made with gin) comes from tarragon, an herb that grows in the hills of Provence.

Ice
2 ounces vodka
1 ounce Tarragon Syrup (below)
¾ ounce fresh lime juice
1 lime wheel

Fill a cocktail shaker with ice. Add the vodka, Tarragon Syrup and lime juice and shake well. Strain into a chilled martini glass and garnish with the lime wheel.

TARRAGON SYRUP In a small saucepan, bring 4 ounces water to a boil with ½ cup sugar. Remove from the heat and add 1 large tarragon sprig. Let cool completely, then strain into an airtight container and refrigerate for up to 1 week. Makes about 6 ounces.

HIBISCUS PETAL
"Taxi" tumbler by Richard Ginori.

hibiscus petal

LANTERN,
CHAPEL HILL, NC

Many of Lantern's cocktails, including the citrusy, basil-spiked Hibiscus Petal, echo the powerful Asian flavors favored by chef-owner Andrea Reusing.

5	small Thai basil leaves, plus 1 Thai basil sprig
½	ounce fresh orange juice
½	ounce fresh lime juice
½	ounce Simple Syrup (p. 14)
Ice	
2	ounces Hibiscus Vodka (below)

In a cocktail shaker, muddle the basil leaves with the orange and lime juices and the Simple Syrup. Add ice and the Hibiscus Vodka and shake well. Strain into an ice-filled rocks glass and garnish with the basil sprig.

HIBISCUS VODKA In a jar, combine 4 ounces vodka with 1 teaspoon dried hibiscus flowers. Let stand for 2 hours, then strain into an airtight container and refrigerate for up to 1 week. Makes 4 ounces.

mandarin & jasmine tea martini

KUMO,
LOS ANGELES

Drink consultant Simon Ford's Mandarin & Jasmine Tea Martini was inspired by cocktail pioneer Audrey Saunders's Earl Grey Marteani, made with tea-infused gin, lemon juice and egg white.

1½ ounces Jasmine Tea–Mandarin Vodka (below)
1 ounce Simple Syrup (p. 14)
¾ ounce fresh lemon juice
3 dashes of orange bitters
1 large egg white

Ice

1 edible orchid (optional)

In a cocktail shaker, combine all of the ingredients except the ice and orchid and shake well for 10 seconds. Add ice and shake for another 10 seconds. Strain into a chilled coupe and garnish with the orchid.

JASMINE TEA–MANDARIN VODKA
In a jar, combine 6 ounces mandarin vodka and 1 tablespoon jasmine tea leaves. Let steep for 1 hour. Strain into an airtight container and refrigerate for up to 1 week. Makes 6 ounces.

green tea-ni

JADE BAR,
PARADISE VALLEY, AZ

Mixologist Greg Portsche is a fan of Charbay Green Tea Vodka, which is made with rare tea leaves from China's Anhui Province.

Ice
2 ounces sake
1 ounce green tea vodka
½ ounce green tea liqueur
1 lemon twist

Fill a pint glass with ice. Add the sake, vodka and liqueur and stir well. Strain into a chilled martini glass and garnish with the lemon twist.

april in paris

MADURO,
MADISON, WI

A newly released pear vodka was bartender David Wilborn's inspiration for this lightly sweet, licorice-accented drink, which he first made in April 2007.

Ice
2½ ounces pear vodka
½ ounce pastis
½ ounce Mandarine Napoléon or Grand Marnier
1 orange twist

Fill a cocktail shaker with ice. Add the vodka, pastis and Mandarine Napoléon and shake well. Strain into a chilled martini glass and garnish with the orange twist.

orange blossom

CRUSTACEAN, LOS ANGELES

Author and cocktail consultant Nick Mautone created this drink in honor of Crustacean's 10th anniversary. The multi-culti cocktail combines lavender from Hawaii, Mandarine Napoléon from Belgium and blood orange juice from Italy.

Ice

2 lemon wedges

1½ ounces orange vodka

½ ounce Cherry Heering or other cherry liqueur

½ ounce Mandarine Napoléon or Grand Marnier

½ ounce fresh orange juice, preferably blood orange

¼ teaspoon ground anise

1 fresh lavender sprig (optional)

Fill a cocktail shaker with ice. Squeeze the juice from the lemon wedges into the shaker and drop them in. Add all of the remaining ingredients except the lavender sprig and shake well. Double strain (p. 17) into a chilled martini glass and garnish with the lavender sprig.

les fesses rouges #2

ENOTECA VIN,
RALEIGH, NC

Having never seen a cocktail made with the aperitif Lillet rouge, bar manager Brad Farran set out to invent one. He played up the red (*rouge*) color with pomegranate juice because "above all, a drink has to look pretty."

Ice
1½ ounces orange vodka
¾ ounce Lillet rouge
¾ ounce pomegranate juice
¾ ounce fresh orange juice
1 orange twist

Fill a cocktail shaker with ice. Add all of the remaining ingredients except the twist and shake well. Strain into a chilled coupe and garnish with the orange twist.

east meets west

CRAFT,
LOS ANGELES

West Coast native and beverage director David Lusby designed the drink menu for New York City star chef Tom Colicchio's new L.A. restaurant. This East-West cocktail gets Asian flavors from lychees and Buddha's Hand citrus.

2 whole strawberries, plus
   1 strawberry slice
2 canned lychees, drained
¾ ounce fresh lemon juice
Ice
1½ ounces citrus vodka,
   preferably Hangar One
   Citron "Buddha's Hand"
¾ ounce Grand Marnier

In a cocktail shaker, muddle the 2 whole strawberries with the lychees and lemon juice. Add ice and the vodka and Grand Marnier and shake well. Strain into a chilled coupe and garnish with the strawberry slice.

lemony laurel

RESTAURANT EVE,
ALEXANDRIA, VA

After tasting a dish of chicken, roasted lemons, bay leaf and a touch of anise at another D.C.–area restaurant, bar manager Todd Thrasher worked the flavors into a drink for Restaurant Eve. The magic ingredients: Galliano, an anise-scented Italian liqueur, and lemons roasted with bay leaves.

Crushed ice
1½ ounces citrus vodka
¾ ounce Galliano
2½ ounces Roasted-Lemon Syrup (below)
1 fresh bay leaf (optional)

Fill a highball glass with crushed ice. Add the vodka, Galliano and Roasted-Lemon Syrup. Using a swizzle stick or a bar spoon turned between both hands, swizzle for 8 seconds. Garnish with the bay leaf.

ROASTED-LEMON SYRUP Halve 5 lemons and remove the seeds. Make 2 slits along the membranes of each half and stuff a dried bay leaf into each slit. Set the lemons cut side up on a baking sheet and bake in a 250° oven for 2 hours. Transfer the roasted lemons to a glass measuring cup and add 12 ounces Simple Syrup (p. 14). Cover and refrigerate overnight. Strain the syrup into an airtight container, squeezing the juice from each lemon, and refrigerate for up to 1 week. Makes about 16 ounces.

LEMONY LAUREL
*"Zombie" glass by Kikatsu
from Eastern Accent.*

celery kamikaze

BEAKER & FLASK,
PORTLAND, OR

Once seen almost exclusively in brunch cocktails like the Bloody Mary, savory ingredients such as the celery juice and pepper vodka in bar owner Kevin Ludwig's kamikaze are making their way into drinks that can be sipped at night.

1 lime wedge and kosher salt
Ice
2 ounces pepper vodka
1 ounce fresh lime juice
1 ounce celery juice
½ ounce Cointreau or other triple sec
½ ounce Simple Syrup (p. 14)

Moisten half of the outer rim of a coupe with the lime wedge and coat lightly with salt. Fill a cocktail shaker with ice and add all of the remaining ingredients; shake well. Strain into the prepared coupe.

zydeco cocktail

TRES AGAVES,
SAN FRANCISCO

Proceeds from sales of Absolut New Orleans, the limited-edition mango and black pepper vodka used in this drink, are donated to charities helping with the city's reconstruction.

4 strawberries, 3 quartered
¼ ounce passion fruit nectar
2 dashes of Peychaud's bitters
Ice
1 ounce Absolut New Orleans
1 ounce Grand Marnier
1 mint sprig

In a cocktail shaker, muddle the quartered strawberries with the passion fruit nectar and bitters. Add ice and the Absolut New Orleans and Grand Marnier and shake well. Strain into an ice-filled rocks glass and garnish with the whole strawberry and the mint sprig.

vanilla-cucumber limey

MARTINI MONKEY,
SAN JOSE, CA

A salad of English cucumbers and butter lettuce with a citrusy dressing inspired bar manager Jay Crabb's lime-and-cucumber-spiked drink.

5 peeled English cucumber wheels
4 mint leaves, plus 1 mint sprig
¾ ounce Simple Syrup (p. 14)
Ice
1½ ounces vanilla vodka
1 ounce fresh lime juice
1½ ounces chilled club soda

In a cocktail shaker, muddle 4 of the cucumber wheels with the mint leaves and Simple Syrup. Add ice and the vodka and lime juice and shake well. Strain into an ice-filled highball glass. Stir in the club soda and garnish with the remaining cucumber wheel and the mint sprig.

BATIDA ROSA (LEFT), P. 81
EL VAQUERO, EUGENE, OR
*"Elizabeth" water glass by
Marc Jacobs for Waterford.*

FOG CUTTER, P. 70
FORBIDDEN ISLAND,
ALAMEDA, CA
*"Flora" highball glass
by Salviati.*

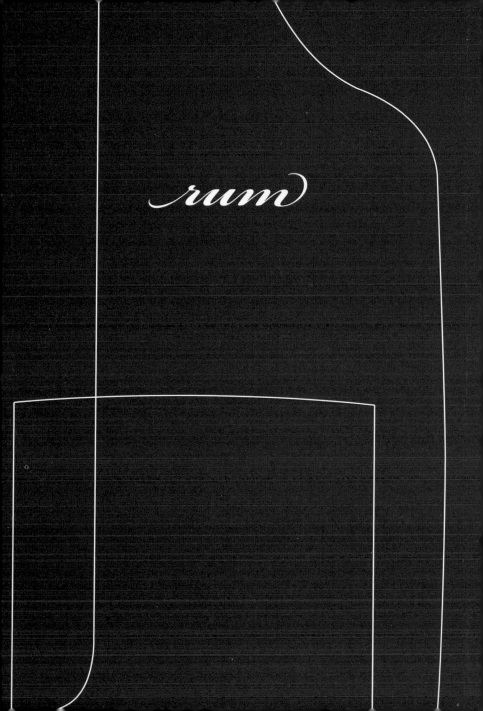

fatty sling

FATTY CRAB,
MANHATTAN

Cocktail expert David Wondrich
conceived the Fatty Sling as a
nod to Donn Beach, the famous
owner of the tiki-themed
restaurant Don the Beachcomber.
Beach, Wondrich says, "liked
combining dashes of Pernod and
Angostura bitters to give
his concoctions a *je ne sais quoi.*"

Ice
1½ ounces overproof white rum
2 ounces pineapple juice
¼ teaspoon Pernod
2 dashes of Angostura bitters
2 ounces chilled ginger ale
1 pineapple wedge and
1 maraschino cherry
1 cocktail umbrella (optional)

Fill a cocktail shaker with ice.
Add the rum, pineapple juice,
Pernod and Angostura bitters
and shake well. Strain into an ice-
filled collins glass and stir in the
chilled ginger ale. Garnish with
the pineapple wedge, maraschino
cherry and cocktail umbrella.

cane juice

BOA STEAKHOUSE,
LAS VEGAS

Fruit preserves are an increasingly popular alternative to simple syrup in cocktails. Here, apricot jam adds both sweetness and an amplified dose of the fresh fruit's faintly tangy, almost musky flavor.

1 lemon wedge and cinnamon sugar (a mixture of 3 tablespoons superfine sugar and 1 teaspoon ground cinnamon)

Ice

2 ounces white rum
1½ ounces fresh lemon juice
½ ounce chilled brewed chai
1½ teaspoons apricot preserves
¼ ounce Grand Marnier
1 dried apricot

Moisten half of the outer rim of a martini glass with the lemon wedge and coat lightly with cinnamon sugar. Fill a cocktail shaker with ice. Add the rum, lemon juice, chai and apricot preserves and shake well. Strain into the prepared martini glass. Pour the Grand Marnier on top and garnish with the dried apricot.

rum

rhuby daiquiri

CHICK'S CAFE & WINE BAR,
PHILADELPHIA

A slice of rhubarb pie gave bartender Katie Loeb the idea for this Floridita Daiquiri variation. "Tweaking a daiquiri with rhubarb seemed like a good starting point," she says. "Ginger and Chinese five-spice powder take the drink to the next level."

Ice

2	ounces white *rhum agricole* (aromatic West Indian rum)
¼	ounce maraschino liqueur
1	ounce fresh pink grapefruit juice
¾	ounce Rhubarb Syrup (below)
¾	ounce fresh lime juice
1	lime wedge

Fill a cocktail shaker with ice. Add all of the remaining ingredients except the lime wedge and shake well. Strain into a chilled coupe and garnish with the lime wedge.

RHUBARB SYRUP In a medium saucepan, bring 2 cups diced rhubarb, 10 ounces water and ¾ cup sugar to a boil. Cover and simmer over low heat until the rhubarb breaks down, about 25 minutes. Remove from the heat. Stir in 1 scant teaspoon grated fresh ginger and a pinch of Chinese five-spice powder and let cool. Strain into an airtight container, pressing on the solids. Refrigerate for up to 1 week. Makes about 12 ounces.

RHUBY DAIQUIRI
"Pinwheel" coupe by Kim Seybert; "Ribbon" carafe from notNeutral.

fog cutter

FORBIDDEN ISLAND,
ALAMEDA, CA

The Fog Cutter is a classic concoction from the legendary Victor "Trader Vic" Bergeron. Forbidden Island owner Martin Cate not only serves the tiki drink at his bar, he's also the registered owner of California license plate FGCUTTR.

Ice

1½ ounces white rum
½ ounce gin
½ ounce brandy
2 ounces fresh orange juice
1 ounce fresh lemon juice
½ ounce orgeat (almond-flavored syrup)
½ ounce Amontillado sherry
1 mint sprig

Fill a cocktail shaker with ice. Add the white rum, gin, brandy, orange and lemon juices and orgeat and shake well. Strain into an ice-filled highball glass and carefully pour the Amontillado sherry on top. Garnish with the mint sprig.

admiral big nose's polynesian delight

**VERVE,
SOMERVILLE, NJ**

A visit to Tahiti, where wild hibiscus flowers bloom everywhere, inspired drink consultant Tad Carducci to create this tiki cocktail. He named it after an imaginary pirate he invented and dubbed Big Nose.

Ice
½ ounce Hibiscus Rum (below)
¾ ounce macadamia liqueur
  or Frangelico
¾ ounce fresh lime juice
½ ounce Velvet Falernum
  (clove-spiced liqueur)
Dash of orange flower water
Pinch of ground allspice
½ orange wheel
1 edible orchid (optional)

Fill a cocktail shaker with ice. Add all of the remaining ingredients except the allspice, orange wheel and orchid and shake well. Strain into an ice-filled rocks glass. Sprinkle the drink with the allspice and garnish with the orange wheel half and orchid.

HIBISCUS RUM In a jar, combine 8 ounces amber rum and 1 tablespoon dried hibiscus flowers and let stand for 30 minutes. Strain through a coffee filter into an airtight container and refrigerate for up to 1 week. Makes 8 ounces.

haitian apricot

PROVENCE,
MANHATTAN

Bar manager Tom Jowett picks up seasonal ingredients for his cocktails at the farmers' market each week. Last summer he sweetened fresh apricots with honey, but apricot preserves can be substituted for the fresh fruit.

Ice
2 ounces amber rum
¾ ounce fresh lime juice
½ ounce Honey Syrup (p. 49)
¼ ounce apricot brandy
1 teaspoon apricot preserves

Fill a cocktail shaker with ice. Add all of the remaining ingredients and shake well. Strain into a chilled martini glass.

golden age

THE VIOLET HOUR,
CHICAGO

While unpacking rarely used bottles of booze the day before the lounge opened, co-owner and bartender Toby Maloney took time to concoct this drink with Cherry Heering in what fellow owner Jason Cott calls "a mad flash of inspiration."

2 ounces amber rum
½ ounce Cherry Heering or other cherry liqueur
¾ ounce fresh lemon juice
½ ounce Simple Syrup (p. 14)
1 large egg yolk
5 dashes of lemon bitters
Ice cubes, plus crushed ice
1 lemon wheel skewered on a pick with 1 maraschino cherry

In a cocktail shaker, combine all of the ingredients except the ice and the garnish; shake for 10 seconds. Add ice cubes and shake for 10 more seconds. Strain into a crushed ice–filled highball glass and garnish with the lemon wheel and cherry.

GOLDEN AGE
*"Pulse" glass by
Calvin Klein.*

ewing no. 33

GREEN STREET,
CAMBRIDGE, MA

Dylan Black doesn't invent many cocktails for his Cambridge restaurant, but he decided that basketball great Patrick Ewing, who grew up within blocks of Green Street, deserved one. Black uses Jamaican rum to honor Ewing's island birthplace, Kingston.

¼ ounce pastis
Ice
2 ounces amber rum
½ ounce Fernet-Branca (bitter Italian digestif)
¼ ounce Spiced Brown Sugar Syrup (below)
Dash of Angostura bitters
1 lime wedge

Rinse a chilled coupe with the pastis, then pour it out. Fill a pint glass with ice. Add all of the remaining ingredients except the lime wedge and stir well. Strain into the prepared coupe and garnish with the lime wedge.

SPICED BROWN SUGAR SYRUP In a saucepan, bring 8 ounces water to a boil with 1 cup dark brown sugar, 1 star anise pod and 2 allspice berries. Simmer over moderate heat for 5 minutes. Let cool, then strain into an airtight container and refrigerate for up to 2 weeks. Makes about 12 ounces.

añejo highball

STAGE LEFT,
NEW BRUNSWICK, NJ

"Curaçao, lime and rum are the Holy Trinity of the island rum drink," says world-famous mixologist Dale DeGroff. His _añejo_ (aged) highball is a tribute to great Cuban bartenders like Constantine Ribalaigua, who created the Papa Doble daiquiri for Hemingway. The Grand Marnier here replaces the curaçao.

Ice
1½ ounces aged amber rum
¾ ounce Grand Marnier
¾ ounce fresh lime juice
2 dashes of Angostura bitters
1 ounce chilled ginger beer
1 lime wheel
½ orange wheel

Fill a cocktail shaker with ice. Add the rum, Grand Marnier, lime juice and bitters and shake well. Strain into an ice-filled highball glass and stir in the ginger beer. Garnish with the lime wheel and orange wheel half.

puerto de cuba

BOURBON & BRANCH,
SAN FRANCISCO

Dominic Venegas uses a vanilla-infused liqueur to play up the underlying vanilla flavors of the port and the aged Cuban-style rum in this drink.

Ice
2 ounces aged amber rum
1 ounce Tawny port
½ ounce Navan (vanilla-flavored brandy-based liqueur)

Fill a pint glass with ice. Add the rum, port and Navan and stir well. Strain into a chilled coupe.

hurricane's eye

PRIMEHOUSE NEW YORK,
MANHATTAN

Mixologist Eben Klemm's tropical cocktail, named after the oddly bright center of a hurricane, is an unexpected departure from the traditional drinks served in most steak houses.

1 tablespoon Rum-Soaked
  Pineapple (below)
2 ounces Pineapple Rum (below)
2 dashes of peach bitters
Crushed ice
1 ounce chilled *aranciata* (Italian
  orange soda) or Orangina
2 pineapple leaves

In a blender, puree the Rum-Soaked Pineapple with the Pineapple Rum and bitters. Pour into a crushed ice–filled red wine glass and stir in the *aranciata*. Garnish with the pineapple leaves.

PINEAPPLE RUM AND RUM-SOAKED PINEAPPLE In a jar, combine 1½ cups demerara sugar, ¼ cup finely diced fresh pineapple and 18 ounces aged *rhum agricole*. Stir to dissolve as much of the sugar as possible. Cover and refrigerate overnight. Strain into an airtight container, reserving some of the pineapple for the drink. Refrigerate for up to 1 week. Makes about 18 ounces.

golden lillet martini

The Edison's owners had old Hollywood in mind when they opened this bar in 2007, with a drink menu (and dress code) reminiscent of legendary Los Angeles nightspots like the Cocoanut Grove and Ciro's.

1 lemon wedge and 2 tablespoons dark brown sugar

Ice

2 ounces aged *rhum agricole* (aromatic West Indian rum)

1½ ounces Lillet blanc

¼ ounce limoncello

1 lemon twist

Moisten half of the outer rim of a martini glass with the lemon wedge and coat lightly with brown sugar. Fill a pint glass with ice. Add the rum, Lillet blanc and limoncello and stir well. Strain into the prepared martini glass and garnish with the lemon twist.

alsatian daiquiri

Owner and star bartender Duggan McDonnell considers spiced rum and Gewürztraminer to be an obvious pairing— the wine's natural pepperiness balances the fragrant rum.

Ice

2 ounces vanilla spiced rum

1 ounce Gewürztraminer

1 ounce fresh lime juice

¾ ounce Simple Syrup (p. 14)

Dash of peach bitters

Fill a cocktail shaker with ice. Add all of the remaining ingredients and shake well. Strain into a chilled coupe.

thai boxer

CYRUS,
HEALDSBURG, CA

Scott Beattie's cocktails are all made with local produce. Some of the herbs for this drink come from La Bonne Terre, a tiny farm run by Bert and Mary Villemaire about a quarter mile from Beattie's house on the Russian River.

10 Thai basil leaves, plus
   1 Thai basil sprig
10 mint leaves
10 cilantro leaves
½ ounce Simple Syrup (p. 14)
Ice
1½ ounces vanilla rum, preferably
   Charbay Tahitian Vanilla Rum
½ ounce unsweetened coconut milk
½ ounce fresh lime juice
1 ounce chilled ginger beer

In a cocktail shaker, muddle the basil leaves with the mint, cilantro and Simple Syrup. Add ice and the rum, coconut milk and lime juice and shake well. Strain into an ice-filled white wine glass or highball glass and stir in the ginger beer. Garnish with the basil sprig.

THAI BOXER
"Joie" iced beverage glass by Monique Lhuillier for Royal Doulton.

rum

the ipanema

**MK,
CHICAGO**

Sommelier Josh Kaplan contributed this cocktail—perfected with the help of MK's pastry chef—to the restaurant's drink list. A lover of cachaça, Kaplan pays tribute to Brazil's most popular spirit with his Ipanema.

Ice
2 ounces cachaça (potent Brazilian sugarcane spirit)
1 ounce apricot nectar
¾ ounce fresh lime juice
¾ ounce Madeira, preferably Sercial
1 lime wheel

Fill a cocktail shaker with ice. Add all of the remaining ingredients except the lime wheel and shake well. Strain into a chilled martini glass and garnish with the lime wheel.

ajilimo

**LA COFRADIA,
CORAL GABLES, FL**

Although *ají limo*—a fragrant hot red pepper—is most often used in ceviche, the bartenders at this Mediterranean-Peruvian restaurant also add it to some of their cocktails for a spicy kick.

Ice
1½ ounces cachaça (potent Brazilian sugarcane spirit)
1 ounce fresh lime juice
½ ounce Simple Syrup (p. 14)
½ teaspoon minced fresh ginger
½-inch chile slice, preferably *ají limo*
4 thyme sprigs

Fill a cocktail shaker with ice. Add the cachaça, lime juice, Simple Syrup, ginger, chile and leaves from 2 of the thyme sprigs; shake well. Strain into an ice-filled rocks glass and garnish with the remaining 2 thyme sprigs.

batida rosa

EL VAQUERO,
EUGENE, OR

When a Brazilian soccer team stopped in to El Vaquero for caipirinhas one night, bartender Jeffrey Morgenthaler came up with this drink to tempt them away from his declining supply of limes.

Ice

2 ounces cachaça (potent Brazilian sugarcane spirit)
1 ounce pineapple juice
1 ounce fresh lemon juice
¾ ounce grenadine, preferably homemade (p. 14)
½ ounce Simple Syrup (p. 14)
3 ounces chilled club soda
1 pineapple spear

Fill a cocktail shaker with ice. Add the cachaça, pineapple juice, lemon juice, grenadine and Simple Syrup. Shake well and strain into a large ice-filled red wine glass. Stir in the club soda and garnish with the pineapple spear.

BLUEBERRIES GONE WILD, P. 91
THE DRAWING ROOM, CHICAGO
*"Spin" tumbler by Arik Levy
for Baccarat.*

gin

gin

ten grand martini

**FORD'S FILLING STATION,
LOS ANGELES**

This fruity martini doesn't cost ten grand, but the addition of pineapple juice makes it look like gold.

Ice
2½ ounces gin
½ ounce Grand Marnier
½ ounce pineapple juice

Fill a pint glass with ice. Add all of the remaining ingredients and stir well. Strain the drink into a chilled martini glass.

gin lane

**TRINA,
FORT LAUDERDALE**

"Gin Lane" refers to William Hogarth's famous 18th-century engraving depicting the evils of London's "gin craze." Gin *and* sloe gin, a sweet red liqueur made from the sloe berry, or blackthorn plum, flavor this potent cocktail.

3 lemon wedges and superfine sugar
2 dashes of Angostura bitters
Ice
1 ounce gin
1 ounce sloe gin, preferably Plymouth
½ ounce sweet vermouth
½ ounce Cointreau or other triple sec
1 lemon twist

Moisten half of the outer rim of a martini glass with 1 of the lemon wedges and coat lightly with sugar. In a cocktail shaker, muddle the remaining 2 lemon wedges with the bitters. Add ice and all of the remaining ingredients except the twist. Shake well and strain into the prepared martini glass. Garnish with the lemon twist.

self-starter cocktail

VESSEL,
SEATTLE

Bartender Jamie Boudreau adapted the Self-Starter from Harry Craddock's recipe in the 1930 *Savoy Cocktail Book.* Craddock's advice on how to drink a cocktail: "Quickly, while it's laughing at you!"

¼ ounce absinthe or Pernod
Ice
1½ ounces gin
¾ ounce Lillet blanc
¼ ounce apricot brandy

Rinse a chilled coupe with the absinthe, then pour it out. Fill a pint glass with ice. Add all of the remaining ingredients and stir well. Strain into the prepared coupe.

hendrick's & honeydew

JAMES,
PHILADELPHIA

Honeydew melon was in season when Kristina Burke and her husband, chef Jim Burke, opened their restaurant, so they decided to use it in a drink. The cucumber and rose flavors in Hendrick's gin balance the melon's almost unctuous sweetness.

7 medium honeydew melon balls
1½ ounces gin, preferably Hendrick's
Ice
1 ounce chilled tonic water
1 thyme sprig

In a cocktail shaker, muddle 4 of the honeydew balls with the gin. Add ice and shake well. Strain into an ice-filled rocks glass and stir in the chilled tonic water. Garnish with the remaining 3 honeydew balls and the thyme sprig.

gin

rose marie

**PIEDMONT,
DURHAM, NC**

When he's not busy curing meats at Piedmont, chef Drew Brown concocts new additions for the restaurant's cocktail list. This rosemary-infused drink is named after Brown's favorite Slim Whitman song.

Ice
2 ounces gin
1 ounce fresh grapefruit juice
½ ounce Rosemary Syrup (below)
1 rosemary sprig

Fill a cocktail shaker with ice. Add the gin, grapefruit juice and Rosemary Syrup; shake well. Strain into a chilled martini glass and garnish with the rosemary sprig.

ROSEMARY SYRUP In a heat-proof bowl, pour 12 ounces hot Simple Syrup (p. 14) over a 4-inch rosemary sprig. Let cool completely. Strain into an airtight container and refrigerate for up to 2 weeks. Makes 12 ounces.

chamomile-teani

BOSTON**

Tea-based cocktails are showing up all over the country. At 33, where the bar is lit by LED panels that can morph into any of 16.7 million colors, they serve a berry-tea martini as well as this honey-accented drink.

Ice
- 1 ounce gin
- ½ ounce Bärenjäger (honey liqueur)
- 2 ounces chilled brewed chamomile tea
- ½ ounce fresh lemon juice
- 1 lemon twist

Fill a cocktail shaker with ice. Add all of the remaining ingredients except the twist and shake well. Strain into a chilled martini glass and garnish with the lemon twist.

87 ways

**TILLMAN'S ROADHOUSE,
DALLAS**

Lucy Brennan, who owns Mint/820 in Portland, Oregon, and consults on Tillman's drink menu, thinks that floral ingredients, like the lavender in this cocktail, deserve more attention behind the bar.

Ice
- 2 ounces gin
- ¼ ounce fresh lemon juice
- ½ ounce Simple Syrup (p. 14)
- ¾ ounce apricot nectar
- 3 dashes of peach bitters
- ¼ teaspoon dried lavender
- 1 fresh lavender sprig (optional)

Fill a cocktail shaker with ice. Add all of the remaining ingredients except the lavender sprig and shake well. Double strain (p. 17) into a chilled martini glass and garnish with the lavender sprig.

lemon & basil martini

PUBLIC,
MANHATTAN

Naren Young created this martini variation after tasting a lemon-and-basil sorbet at a restaurant. Sweet white vermouth emphasizes the basil's herbal quality, while limoncello and lemon juice give the drink a double-citrus punch.

3   basil leaves, plus 1 basil sprig
¼   ounce Simple Syrup (p. 14)
Ice
2   ounces gin
½   ounce limoncello
½   ounce bianco vermouth
     (sweet white vermouth)
½   ounce fresh lemon juice

In a cocktail shaker, muddle the basil leaves with the Simple Syrup. Add ice and all of the remaining ingredients except the sprig; shake well. Strain into a chilled martini glass and garnish with the sprig.

parsley gin julep

IRIS,
NEW ORLEANS

Bartender Alan Walter remembers the genesis of this refreshing drink: "It was summer. I had already used up the restaurant's supply of fruit and was looking for a new ingredient. Half an hour later the chef, Ian Schnoebelen, asked, 'Hey, what did you do with the parsley?'"

8   parsley leaves
¾   ounce fresh lime juice
¾   ounce Simple Syrup (p. 14)
Ice cubes, plus crushed ice
1½ ounces gin
1   ounce chilled club soda
1   lime wheel

In a cocktail shaker, muddle the parsley with the lime juice and Simple Syrup. Add ice cubes and the gin and shake well. Strain into a crushed ice–filled collins glass. Stir in the club soda and garnish with the lime wheel.

LEMON & BASIL
MARTINI (LEFT)
*Martini glass
from Crate & Barrel.*

PARSLEY GIN JULEP
*"Colombina" Champagne
flute from Alessi.*

honey don't

SOUTH,
RALEIGH, NC

This drink started as a gin martini;
then partner John Lambrakis
consulted pastry chef Eric Akbari,
who suggested adding melon granita
to make it more refreshing. The
result, according to Lambrakis, was a
cocktail that says "summer."

2 unpeeled cucumber wheels
1 mint sprig
½ ounce Simple Syrup (p. 14)
Ice
2 ounces gin
3 tablespoons Honeydew Granita
   (below)
¾ ounce fresh lemon juice

In a cocktail shaker, muddle 1 of
the cucumber wheels with the mint
and Simple Syrup. Add ice and
the gin, Honeydew Granita and lemon
juice and shake well. Strain into
a chilled martini glass and float
the remaining cucumber wheel on
the surface of the drink.

HONEYDEW GRANITA In a blender,
puree the flesh from ¼ medium
honeydew melon with 1 ounce
Simple Syrup (p. 14), 2 mint leaves,
1 teaspoon Midori, a pinch of salt
and ¼ ounce each of fresh orange
juice and fresh lemon juice. Transfer
to a small, shallow pan and freeze,
stirring with a fork every 15 minutes,
until the texture is icy and flaky, about
1½ hours. The granita can be kept
in the freezer for up to 1 week; if it
becomes solid, chop into chunks and
puree in a food processor until fluffy.
Makes about 3 cups.

blueberries gone wild

THE DRAWING ROOM,
CHICAGO

Health-conscious bar chef Debbi
Peek created this gin drink
to showcase antioxidant-dense
ingredients, including
blueberries and pomegranate.

11 blueberries, 3 skewered on a pick
¼ ounce fresh lemon juice
¼ ounce agave nectar
Ice cubes, plus crushed ice
1½ ounces gin
½ ounce pomegranate liqueur
1 lemon wheel

In a cocktail shaker, muddle
8 blueberries with the lemon juice
and agave nectar. Add ice cubes
and the gin and pomegranate
liqueur and shake well. Strain into
a crushed ice–filled rocks glass
and garnish with the skewered
blueberries and the lemon wheel.

green lantern

RANGE,
SAN FRANCISCO

Range features a nightly
cocktail special. In this drink,
bartender Thomas Waugh
pairs kiwi with flowery Viognier
and just-squeezed lime juice.

½ kiwi, peeled and diced
¼ ounce Simple Syrup (p. 14)
Ice
1½ ounces gin
1 ounce Viognier
½ ounce fresh lime juice

In a cocktail shaker, muddle
the kiwi with the Simple Syrup.
Add ice and the gin, Viognier
and lime juice and shake well.
Strain into a chilled martini glass.

THE UN-USUAL SUSPECT

*"Colette" Champagne
saucers by Marc Jacobs
for Waterford.*

the un-usual suspect

CANLIS,
SEATTLE

Bartender Kai Braaten offers the Un-Usual Suspect as an alternative to the Negroni, another pleasantly bitter aperitif cocktail. Both drinks use Italian bitters, but Braaten prefers Fernet-Branca's herbal complexity to the Campari in Negronis for this drink.

Ice
1½ ounces gin
¾ ounce fresh grapefruit juice
½ ounce Drambuie
½ ounce Honey Syrup (p. 49)
¼ ounce fresh lemon juice
⅛ ounce Fernet-Branca
Dash of Angostura bitters
1 grapefruit twist

Fill a cocktail shaker with ice. Add all of the remaining ingredients except the twist and shake well. Strain the drink into a chilled coupe and garnish with the grapefruit twist.

long live the queen

ECCO,
ATLANTA

Head bartender Seth Schiendeldecker had a hunch that the subtle scent of elderflowers would be perfect with the juniper flavors in gin. Long Live the Queen proves that he was right.

Ice
1¾ ounces gin
½ ounce elderflower liqueur
¾ ounce fresh lemon juice
¼ ounce Simple Syrup (p. 14)
2 dashes of peach bitters
4 mint leaves
1 lemon twist

Fill a cocktail shaker with ice. Add all of the remaining ingredients except the twist and shake well. Double strain (p. 17) into a chilled coupe and garnish with the lemon twist.

violet fizz

TAILOR,
MANHATTAN

Before importer Eric Seed
reintroduced crème de violette
to the U.S. market last year,
American bartenders like Tailor's
Eben Freeman purchased
the hard-to-find liqueur in London
or Paris and packed it in their
carry-on luggage to bring home.

2 ounces gin
½ ounce fresh lemon juice
½ ounce fresh lime juice
¼ ounce Simple Syrup (p. 14)
½ ounce crème de violette
(violet-flavored liqueur)
½ ounce half-and-half
1 large egg white
Ice
2 ounces chilled club soda
1 fresh edible violet or crushed
candied violets (optional)

In a cocktail shaker, combine
all of the ingredients except the
ice, club soda and violet. Shake
well for 10 seconds. Add ice
and shake for 10 more seconds.
Strain the drink into a chilled
highball glass, top with the club
soda and garnish with the violet.

gin-esaisquoi

WHITE MOUNTAIN CIDER CO.,
GLEN, NH

This drink, which gets its frothy texture from being shaken with an egg white, was named for bartender Jeff Grdinich's best friend, Kevin Ginestet, who, ironically, is allergic to eggs and doesn't drink alcohol.

1 large egg white
1½ ounces gin
1½ ounces Lillet blanc
¾ ounce Velvet Falernum (clove-spiced liqueur)
2 dashes of orange bitters, preferably Regan's
Ice
Pinch of ground cardamom

In a cocktail shaker, combine all of the ingredients except the ice and cardamom and shake for 10 seconds. Add ice and shake for 10 more seconds. Strain into a chilled coupe and sprinkle with the cardamom.

opera cocktail

ENCORE LIQUID LOUNGE,
CHICAGO

The Hotel Allegro's Encore Liquid Lounge features classic drinks such as the Opera Cocktail, which was served at Harry's New York Bar in Paris during the 1920s.

Ice
2 ounces gin
¾ ounce Dubonnet rouge
¼ ounce maraschino liqueur
Dash of orange bitters
1 lemon twist

Fill a pint glass with ice. Add all of the remaining ingredients except the twist and stir well. Strain into a chilled coupe and garnish with the lemon twist.

gin

straits sling

XIX NINETEEN CAFÉ,
PHILADELPHIA

According to cocktail historian
Ted Haigh, the dry, refreshingly
bitter Straits Sling originated at
the Long Bar of Singapore's
Raffles Hotel around 1915. It was
reformulated into the sweeter,
more tropical Singapore Sling
sometime between 1922 and 1930.

Ice
2 ounces gin
½ ounce kirsch (cherry eau-de-vie)
½ ounce Bénédictine (brandy-
based herbal liqueur)
2 dashes of orange bitters
2 dashes of Angostura bitters
1½ ounces chilled club soda
¼ orange wheel and
1 brandied cherry

Fill a cocktail shaker with ice.
Add the gin, kirsch, Bénédictine
and both bitters and shake well.
Strain into an ice-filled collins
glass. Stir in the chilled club soda
and garnish with the orange wheel
quarter and the brandied cherry.

FOOD & WINE · 96 · COCKTAILS 2008

STRAITS SLING

*"Zombie" glass
by Kikatsu
from Eastern
Accent.*

the trois cocktail

**TROIS,
ATLANTA**

The martini atomizer, popular in the 1950s and '60s, when bone-dry martinis required only a misting of vermouth, is repurposed at Trois by mixologist Eric Simpkins, who uses it to add the aroma of rose water without overpowering the drink.

1½ ounces Mint–Green Tea Gin (below)
1 ounce fresh lemon juice
¾ ounce Simple Syrup (p. 14)
1 large egg white
Ice
1 spritz or 2 drops of rose water
1 lemon twist

In a cocktail shaker, combine all of the ingredients except the ice, rose water and twist. Shake well for 10 seconds. Fill the shaker with ice and shake for 10 more seconds. Strain into a chilled coupe. Using a clean atomizer, spray the drink lightly with rose water or add the drops. Garnish with the lemon twist.

MINT–GREEN TEA GIN In a jar, combine 8 ounces gin with 2 green tea bags and 12 mint leaves. Let stand for 2 hours. Strain into an airtight container and refrigerate for up to 1 week. Makes 8 ounces.

cucumber mint creole

PEGU CLUB,
MANHATTAN

Pegu Club co-owner Audrey Saunders used the classic Creole Cocktail—gin, lemon juice and sherry—as the basis for this drink.

2 mint sprigs
4 unpeeled cucumber wheels
¾ ounce fresh lemon juice
½ ounce Simple Syrup (p. 14)
Ice
1½ ounces gin
½ ounce Dry Sack sherry
½ ounce cask-aged aquavit (caraway-flavored distilled spirit), preferably Linie

In a pint glass, muddle the leaves from 1 of the mint sprigs with 3 of the cucumber wheels, the lemon juice and the Simple Syrup. Add ice and the gin, sherry and aquavit and stir well. Double strain (p. 17) the drink into a chilled coupe and garnish with the remaining mint sprig and cucumber wheel.

SUEÑO, P. 102
TEQUILA'S RESTAURANT,
PHILADELPHIA
*"Horizon" highball
glass from Baccarat.*

sueño

10 rosemary leaves, plus
   1 rosemary sprig
 6 very thin unpeeled English
   cucumber wheels
¾ ounce fresh lime juice
½ ounce Simple Syrup (p. 14)
Ice
 2 ounces blanco tequila
 1 ounce chilled tonic water

1. In a cocktail shaker, muddle the rosemary leaves with 3 of the cucumber wheels, the lime juice and the Simple Syrup. Add ice and the tequila and shake well.

2. In a highball glass, layer the remaining 3 cucumber wheels with ice. Strain the drink into the prepared highball glass, gently stir in the tonic and garnish with the rosemary sprig.

strawberry fields

REEF,
HOUSTON

Chef and Beatles fan Bryan Caswell loves fresh ingredients and anything with a licorice taste. For this drink, he muddles fresh strawberries with licorice-scented tarragon.

4   strawberries, 3 quartered
½   tarragon sprig
½   ounce Simple Syrup (p. 14)
Ice
2   ounces blanco tequila
¾   ounce fresh lemon juice

In a cocktail shaker, muddle the quartered strawberries with the tarragon and Simple Syrup. Add ice and the tequila and lemon juice and shake well. Double strain (p. 17) into a chilled martini glass and garnish with the whole strawberry.

ruby slipper

PROVIDENCE,
LOS ANGELES

Bar manager Vincenzo Marianella prefers to use 4 Copas blanco tequila, one of the only organic tequilas on the market, in his Ruby Slipper.

Ice
2   ounces blanco tequila
½   ounce lychee liqueur
¾   ounce fresh pink grapefruit juice
¾   ounce fresh lime juice
½   teaspoon agave nectar
½   small, thin grapefruit wheel

Fill a cocktail shaker with ice. Add all of the remaining ingredients except the grapefruit wheel and shake well. Strain into a chilled coupe and garnish with the grapefruit wheel half.

manzarita

CENTRO,
BOULDER, CO

To give this tequila smash an autumnal feel, bar manager Devlin DeVore adds apple juice ("apple" is *manzana* in Spanish) and cinnamon.

½ lemon, quartered
Pinch of ground cinnamon
Ice
2 ounces blanco tequila
¾ ounce elderflower liqueur
1½ ounces apple juice
1 cinnamon stick

In a cocktail shaker, muddle the lemon quarters with the ground cinnamon. Add ice and the tequila, elderflower liqueur and apple juice and shake well. Strain into an ice-filled rocks glass and garnish with the cinnamon stick.

bella rosa

DEVITO SOUTH BEACH,
MIAMI BEACH

Mixologist Elad Zvi likes working with such Middle Eastern ingredients as almonds, rose petals and fresh pomegranate juice because they remind him of his childhood in Israel.

½ ounce fresh lime juice
½ ounce pomegranate juice
1 ounce blanco tequila
½ ounce elderflower liqueur
½ ounce Lillet blanc
1 large egg white
Ice

In a cocktail shaker, combine all of the ingredients except the ice and shake well for 10 seconds. Add ice and shake again. Strain into an ice-filled rocks glass.

MANZARITA
"TAC 02" double old-fashioned glass from Rosenthal.

guavarita

WHISKNLADLE,
SAN DIEGO

Whisknladle owner Arturo Kassel uses guava nectar and a citrus-spiked salt rim in his riff on the classic margarita.

1 lemon wedge and citrus salt (a mixture of ¼ teaspoon each of finely grated lemon and lime zests and 2 teaspoons kosher salt)

Ice

2 ounces blanco tequila

½ ounce Cointreau or other triple sec

1 ounce guava nectar

½ ounce fresh lime juice

¼ ounce Simple Syrup (p. 14)

Moisten half of the outer rim of a martini glass with the lemon wedge and coat lightly with citrus salt. Fill a cocktail shaker with ice. Add all of the remaining ingredients and shake well. Strain into the prepared martini glass.

mi-so-pretty

ORSON,
SAN FRANCISCO

Orson chef-owner Elizabeth Falkner and mixologist Angie Heeney-Tunstall experiment with savory cocktails like this miso-based drink.

2 teaspoons white miso

3 ounces fresh grapefruit juice

¾ ounce Toasted-Almond Syrup (below)

Ice

1½ ounces blanco tequila

1 orange twist

In a cocktail shaker, stir the miso, grapefruit juice and Toasted-Almond Syrup together. Add ice and the tequila and shake well. Strain into an ice-filled highball glass and garnish with the orange twist.

TOASTED-ALMOND SYRUP
Toast ¼ cup coarsely chopped raw almonds in a 350° oven until golden, about 7 minutes. Pour into a heatproof bowl and add 6 ounces hot Simple Syrup (p. 14). Let cool completely, then strain into an airtight container and refrigerate for up to 2 weeks. Makes 6 ounces.

tequila

bohemio ■

TAILOR,
MANHATTAN

The name of bar manager Eben Freeman's drink refers to Bohemia, the region of the Czech Republic that traditionally produced the bitter liqueur called Becherovka. Becherovka is flavored with a secret blend of herbs and spices.

Ice

2	ounces reposado tequila
¼	ounce mezcal
½	ounce fresh lemon juice
½	ounce fresh orange juice
½	ounce Simple Syrup (p. 14)
½	ounce Becherovka
1	orange twist, flamed (p. 16)

Fill a cocktail shaker with ice. Add the tequila, mezcal, lemon juice, orange juice, Simple Syrup and Becherovka and shake well. Strain into an ice-filled rocks glass and garnish with the flamed orange twist.

socoloco

CAFÉ ADELAIDE &
THE SWIZZLE STICK BAR,
NEW ORLEANS

**Mixologist Lu Brow accents
this drink with Southern
Comfort, a whiskey-
based liqueur invented in
New Orleans in 1874.**

2	lime wedges and kosher salt
Ice	
2	ounces reposado tequila
1	ounce Southern Comfort
¾	ounce fresh lime juice
¼	ounce Simple Syrup (p. 14)

Moisten half of the outer
rim of a coupe with 1 of the
lime wedges and coat lightly
with salt. Fill a cocktail shaker
with ice. Add the tequila,
Southern Comfort, lime juice
and Simple Syrup and shake
well. Strain into the prepared
coupe and garnish with
the remaining lime wedge.

tequila

rojo bianco

DEATH & CO.,
MANHATTAN

Bar manager Philip Ward compares creating new cocktails to playing with Mr. Potato Head's interchangeable features. In this variation on the Brooklyn Cocktail, he substitutes tequila for rye, sweet vermouth for dry and Campari for Amer Picon, a French bitter liqueur.

Ice

2 ounces reposado tequila
¼ ounce bianco vermouth
   (sweet white vermouth)
¼ ounce Campari
¼ ounce maraschino liqueur
Dash of Angostura bitters

Fill a pint glass with ice. Add the tequila, vermouth, Campari, maraschino liqueur and bitters and stir well. Strain into a chilled coupe.

el gusano rojo

THE WHITE HEART,
PORTLAND, ME

This downtown Portland cocktail lounge, which is popular with students from the nearby Maine College of Art, features local art, DJs and live bands.

Ice

1½ ounces mezcal
½ ounce passion fruit nectar
2 ounces chilled ginger beer
½ ounce grenadine, preferably
   homemade (p. 14)

Fill a cocktail shaker with ice. Add the mezcal and passion fruit nectar and shake well. Strain the drink into an ice-filled highball glass, stir in the chilled ginger beer and drizzle the grenadine on top; it will sink to the bottom.

EL GUSANO ROJO
*"Staggered Cut" highball glass
by Calvin Klein.*

BUFALA NEGRA, P. 114
THE OAKROOM, LOUISVILLE, KY
*"Lars" double old-fashioned glass
from Crate & Barrel.*

whiskey

whiskey

ciudad malo

NATT SPIL,
MADISON, WI

Bar manager Michael Reynolds named his Manhattan variation after the local nickname for Madison, Wisconsin—Mad City, roughly "Ciudad Malo" in Spanish.

Ice
2 ounces bourbon
¾ ounce sweet vermouth
2 dashes of Peychaud's bitters
3 drops of orange flower water
1 orange twist skewered on a pick with 1 brandied cherry

Fill a pint glass with ice. Add the bourbon, vermouth, bitters and orange flower water and stir well. Strain into a chilled coupe and garnish with the skewered orange twist and cherry.

bufala negra

THE OAKROOM,
LOUISVILLE, KY

At The Oakroom, where Al Capone regularly played poker in the 1920s, the bartenders use bourbon from Buffalo Trace Distillery in nearby Frankfort, Kentucky.

4 basil leaves
1 teaspoon aged balsamic vinegar
½ ounce Simple Syrup (p. 14)
Ice
1½ ounces bourbon
1½ ounces chilled ginger ale

In a cocktail shaker, muddle 3 of the basil leaves with the vinegar and Simple Syrup. Add ice and the bourbon and shake well. Strain the drink into an ice-filled rocks glass, stir in the ginger ale and garnish with the remaining basil leaf.

pinch of basil

FIREFLY,
WASHINGTON, DC

Executive chef Daniel Bortnick collaborates on all of Firefly's cocktails. His bourbon of choice for this apple-flavored drink is Basil Hayden's Kentucky Straight.

Ice
1½ ounces bourbon
½ ounce Pommeau de Normandie (Calvados aged with apple juice)
2 ounces apple juice
1 thin green apple slice skewered on a pick with 1 small cantaloupe ball and 1 small honeydew ball

Fill a pint glass with ice. Add the bourbon, Pommeau de Normandie and apple juice and stir well. Strain into a chilled martini glass and garnish with the skewered apple slice and melon balls.

miss smith

MAKER'S MARK
BOURBON HOUSE & LOUNGE,
LOUISVILLE, KY

Apple schnapps first became popular at German universities during the 1970s. It's made by blending a neutral grain-based spirit with fresh apple juice.

Ice
2 ounces bourbon, preferably Maker's Mark
1 ounce *apfelkorn* (German apple schnapps)
1 ounce apple juice
1 apple slice

Fill a pint glass with ice. Add all of the remaining ingredients except the apple slice and stir well. Strain into a chilled martini glass and garnish with the apple slice.

BLANCA JULEP
*"Octavia" footed tumbler
by Juliska.*

blanca julep

BLANCA,
SAN DIEGO

Bar manager Jennifer Zerboni likes to tinker with the classic mint julep during horse-racing season. She used to flavor this julep with a mint *granité*, but that proved "too sticky and messy." Now she makes the drink with mint simple syrup.

8	mint leaves, plus 3 mint sprigs
¾	ounce fresh lime juice
½	ounce Simple Syrup (p. 14)
2½	ounces bourbon
1	ounce chilled club soda
1	cup crushed ice
1	lime wedge

In a highball glass, muddle the mint leaves with the lime juice and Simple Syrup. Add the bourbon and club soda, then fill the glass with the crushed ice. Using a swizzle stick or bar spoon turned between both hands, swizzle for 10 seconds. Garnish with the mint sprigs and the lime wedge.

the david carradine martini

BASA,
LOUISVILLE, KY

Basa owner Steven Ton created this drink when he worked at an Asian restaurant called Grasshopper, which happens to be actor David Carradine's nickname in the 1970s TV show *Kung Fu*.

	Ice
2	ounces bourbon
½	ounce Chambord
½	ounce Simple Syrup (p. 14)
¾	ounce fresh lemon juice
1	lemon twist

Fill a cocktail shaker with ice. Add all of the remaining ingredients except the twist and shake well. Strain into a chilled martini glass and garnish with the lemon twist.

matador

AMADA,
PHILADELPHIA

All specialty cocktails at Amada are named after Pedro Almodóvar films. For the violent black comedy *Matador*, bartender Stephen Seibert created this easy-drinking bourbon refresher spiked with candied ginger and a flamed twist.

2	thin fresh ginger slices
¾	ounce fresh lemon juice
¾	ounce elderflower liqueur
2	dashes of orange bitters
Ice	
1½	ounces bourbon
1½	ounces chilled ginger ale
1	orange twist, flamed (p. 16), and 1 candied ginger slice

In a cocktail shaker, muddle the fresh ginger with the lemon juice, liqueur and bitters. Add ice and the bourbon; shake well. Strain into an ice-filled highball glass. Stir in the ginger ale. Garnish with the flamed twist and candied ginger.

tommy gun

BAR DRAKE,
SAN FRANCISCO

Mixologist Jacques Bezuindenhout's sour, which references the iconic firearm wielded by Prohibition-era gangsters, gets its zing from spicy fresh ginger and a generous pour of Irish whiskey.

2	thin fresh ginger slices
1	teaspoon apricot jam
¼	ounce fresh lemon juice
Ice	
2	ounces Irish whiskey
½	ounce Grand Marnier
1	lemon twist

In a cocktail shaker, muddle the ginger with the jam and lemon juice. Add ice and the whiskey and Grand Marnier; shake well. Strain into an ice-filled rocks glass. Garnish with the lemon twist.

TOMMY GUN
"Glacier" glasses by Karen Feldman for Artel.

TENNESSEE ROSE
*"Duchesse" highball glasses by
Vera Wang for Wedgwood.*

tennessee rose

PALEY'S PLACE,
PORTLAND, OR

Mixologist Suzanne Bozarth sweetens this winter whiskey sour with cassis to give it a pink blush. Portland is, after all, known as the Rose City.

Ice

2	ounces Tennessee whiskey
3	ounces fresh grapefruit juice
¾	ounce fresh lemon juice
¼	ounce crème de cassis (black-currant liqueur)
1	lemon wedge

Edible rose petals (optional)

Fill a cocktail shaker with ice. Add all of the remaining ingredients except the lemon wedge and rose petals; shake well. Strain into an ice-filled collins glass. Garnish with the lemon wedge and rose petals.

the stiletto

HUMBLE PIE,
RALEIGH, NC

Cocktail writer Christopher Hirst tracked the origin of The Stiletto to Houston, where bartender Al Romeo added amaretto to his whiskey drink and named it, most agree, after the iconic heel. The bartenders at Humble Pie add cranberry juice to the mix.

Ice

2	ounces Canadian whisky
¾	ounce fresh lemon juice
¾	ounce cranberry juice
½	ounce Simple Syrup (p. 14)
¼	ounce amaretto
1	lemon twist

Fill a cocktail shaker with ice. Add all of the remaining ingredients except the twist and shake well. Strain into a chilled martini glass and garnish with the lemon twist.

whiskey

revival

MONARCH,
ST. LOUIS

The Revival is bar manager Ted Kilgore's homage to the first golden age of cocktails (from the late 1800s until Prohibition)—and "a celebration of the new golden age!" he says.

Ice
- 2 ounces rye whiskey
- ½ ounce Bénédictine (brandy-based herbal liqueur)
- ½ ounce maraschino liqueur
- 2 dashes of absinthe or Pernod
- ¾ ounce fresh lemon juice
- 1 lemon twist

Fill a cocktail shaker with ice. Add all of the remaining ingredients except the twist and shake well. Strain into a chilled martini glass and garnish with the lemon twist.

cooper's cocktail

VESSEL,
SEATTLE

For years, Fernet-Branca, a bitter Italian digestif, has been a favorite shot among West Coast bartenders, who have begun to use it in place of traditional cocktail bitters like Angostura.

Ice
- 2 ounces rye whiskey
- ¾ ounce elderflower liqueur
- ¼ ounce Fernet-Branca
- 1 orange twist

Fill a pint glass with ice. Add all of the remaining ingredients except the twist and stir well. Strain into a chilled coupe and garnish with the orange twist.

remember the maine

**THE GOOD FORK,
BROOKLYN, NY**

Barman St. John Frizell prefers to mix this drink with Carpano Antica Formula, a slightly less sweet vermouth than the one bon vivant Charles H. Baker Jr. calls for in his 1937 drinking treatise, *The Gentleman's Companion, Volume II.*

Ice
2 ounces rye whiskey
¾ ounce Carpano Antica Formula or other sweet vermouth
½ ounce Cherry Heering or other cherry liqueur
½ teaspoon Pernod
1 lemon twist

Fill a pint glass with ice. Add all of the remaining ingredients except the twist and stir well. Strain into a chilled coupe and garnish with the lemon twist.

filibuster cocktail

**FLORA,
OAKLAND, CA**

At Flora, a restaurant located in an Art Deco building in downtown Oakland, consultant Erik Adkins set up a classics-minded cocktail program featuring drinks like this bittersweet whiskey sour.

1½ ounces rye whiskey
¾ ounce fresh lemon juice
¼ ounce pure maple syrup
Dash of Angostura bitters
1 large egg white
Ice
1 lemon twist

Fill a cocktail shaker with all of the ingredients except the ice and the twist and shake well. Add ice and shake again. Strain the drink into a chilled martini glass and garnish with the lemon twist.

whiskey

ortensia

**AMALIA,
MANHATTAN**

For the cocktails at Amalia, beverage director Holly Roberts refashions classic recipes such as the Negroni, made here with Scotch whisky and Punt e Mes, an assertive sweet vermouth.

Ice

1 ounce blended Scotch

1 ounce Punt e Mes or other sweet vermouth

1 ounce Aperol (bitter orange aperitif)

1 orange twist

Fill a pint glass with ice. Add all of the remaining ingredients except the twist and stir well. Strain the drink into an ice-filled rocks glass and garnish with the orange twist.

whiz bang

**CERO RESTAURANT,
FORT LAUDERDALE**

Cero's version of this World War I–era cocktail—published in Robert Vermeire's 1922 *Cocktails: How to Mix Them*—omits the grenadine from the original recipe, resulting in a drink with even more whiz and bang.

Ice

1½ ounces single-malt Scotch

¼ ounce Pernod

¾ ounce dry vermouth

Dash of orange bitters

1 orange twist

Fill a pint glass with ice. Add all of the remaining ingredients except the twist and stir well. Strain the drink into a chilled coupe and garnish with the orange twist.

ORTENSIA

"Vesta" tumbler by William Yeoward.

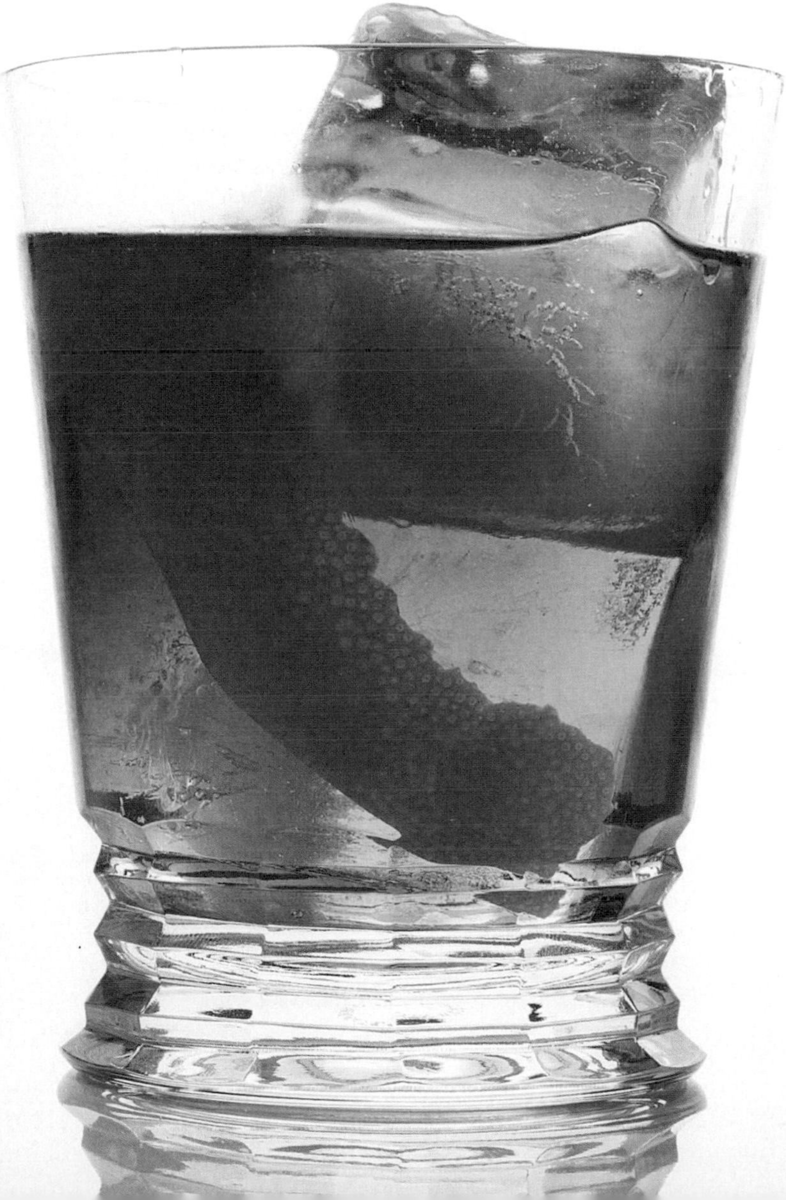

pear shaped

BALABAN'S,
ST. LOUIS

The bartenders at Balaban's prefer pear brandy from Clear Creek, a Portland distillery that uses Oregon fruit to produce traditional Swiss-and Alsace-style eaux-de-vie.

Ice
2 ounces single-malt Scotch
½ ounce Belle de Brillet (pear liqueur)
¾ ounce apple juice
¾ ounce fresh lemon juice
½ ounce Vanilla Syrup (below)

Fill a cocktail shaker with ice. Add all of the remaining ingredients and shake well. Strain into a chilled martini glass.

VANILLA SYRUP In a small saucepan, combine 12 ounces Simple Syrup (p. 14) with ½ vanilla bean and the scraped seeds. Simmer over moderate heat for 5 minutes. Remove from the heat and let cool. Strain into an airtight container and refrigerate for up to 2 weeks. Makes about 10 ounces.

jose mcgregor

LION & COMPASS,
SUNNYVALE, CA

While helping Lion & Compass's pastry chef with a new dessert recipe, bartender Jimmy Patrick accidentally combined Licor 43 and Scotch. They worked well together; Patrick later added bitters to round out the flavor.

Ice
2 ounces single-malt Scotch
½ ounce Licor 43 (citrus-and-vanilla-flavored liqueur)
2 dashes of orange bitters
1 lemon twist

Fill a pint glass with ice. Add the Scotch, Licor 43 and bitters and stir well. Strain into an ice-filled rocks glass and garnish with the lemon twist.

chancellor

LITTLE BRANCH,
MANHATTAN

This drink shows up in Frederic Birmingham's venerable 1956 *Esquire Drink Book*. It's right at home at Little Branch, where co-owner Joseph Schwartz presides as one of the deans of the New York City cocktail scene.

Ice
2 ounces single-malt Scotch
½ ounce Ruby port
½ ounce dry vermouth
Dash of Peychaud's bitters

Fill a pint glass with ice. Add the Scotch, port, vermouth and bitters and stir well. Strain into a chilled coupe.

ACCOUTREMENT, P. 135
ARNAUD'S FRENCH 75 BAR,
NEW ORLEANS
*"Queen" martini glass
by Rosenthal; "Iona" shot
glass from Lekker.*

brandy

brandy

noir sidecar

NOIR BAR,
LAS VEGAS

A secret passageway leads
from an outside entrance into
Noir's candlelit bar, which
serves Ken Hall's extravagant
drink enhanced by pear
eau-de-vie and Bénédictine.

1 lemon wedge and superfine sugar
Ice
1½ ounces Cognac
½ ounce Cointreau or other
triple sec
½ ounce Bénédictine (brandy-based
herbal liqueur)
½ ounce Poire William or other
pear brandy
¾ ounce fresh lemon juice
1 lemon twist

Moisten half of the outer rim
of a martini glass with the lemon
wedge and coat lightly with
superfine sugar. Fill a cocktail
shaker with ice. Add the Cognac,
Cointreau, Bénédictine, Poire
William and lemon juice and shake
well. Strain into the prepared
martini glass and garnish with
the lemon twist.

champs elysées cocktail

ZIG ZAG CAFE,
SEATTLE

The Zig Zag Cafe is known for resurrecting obscure classics. This sophisticated sidecar variation was listed in the 1930 *Savoy Cocktail Book.*

Ice
1½ ounces Cognac
½ ounce green Chartreuse
¼ ounce fresh lemon juice
⅛ ounce Simple Syrup (p. 14)
2 dashes of Angostura bitters

Fill a cocktail shaker with ice. Add all of the remaining ingredients and shake well. Strain into a chilled coupe.

mango djarum

MODUS SUPPER CLUB,
SAN DIEGO

Mixologist Ariana Johnson takes cues from traditional recipes while playing with unusual flavor combinations. Her Mango Djarum revs up a sidecar with spicy cloves and sweet mango.

1 lemon wedge and clove sugar (a mixture of 2 teaspoons superfine sugar and ¼ teaspoon ground cloves)
Ice
1½ ounces Cognac
¾ ounce Cointreau or other triple sec
¾ ounce fresh lemon juice
½ ounce mango nectar

Moisten half of the outer rim of a martini glass with the lemon wedge and coat lightly with clove sugar. Fill a cocktail shaker with ice. Add all of the remaining ingredients and shake well. Strain into the prepared martini glass.

 *brandy*

tahitian moon

HOLEMAN & FINCH
PUBLIC HOUSE,
ATLANTA

Mixologist Greg Best named this cocktail—made with Tahitian vanilla bean—after a song by the alternative rock band Porno for Pyros.

Ice

1½ ounces brandy
½ ounce Oloroso sherry
2 dashes of Angostura bitters
3 ounces chilled vanilla cream soda
1 long lemon twist wrapped around
  1 vanilla bean (optional)

Fill a pint glass with ice. Add the brandy and sherry; stir well. Strain into an ice-filled collins glass and stir in the vanilla soda. Garnish with the twist-wrapped vanilla bean.

sherry cocktail

RAYUELA,
MANHATTAN

For this Iberian sour, bar chef Junior Merino prefers brandy de Jerez, which is made in the same coastal region as sherry.

Ice

1 ounce Palo Cortado or
  Amontillado sherry
1 ounce brandy, preferably Spanish
½ ounce grenadine, preferably
  homemade (p. 14)
¼ ounce fresh lemon juice
¼ ounce Cherry Heering or other
  cherry liqueur
1 orange twist, flamed (p. 16), and
  1 brandied cherry

Fill a cocktail shaker with ice. Add all of the remaining ingredients except the twist and cherry; shake well. Strain into an ice-filled rocks glass. Garnish with the twist and cherry.

SHERRY COCKTAIL
"Smoke" tumbler by Arik Levy
for Baccarat; vase by Salviati.

brandy

the wreck

BENJY'S,
HOUSTON

In his ongoing efforts to bridge the gap between bar and kitchen, mixologist Robert Heugel incorporates a *gastrique*—the classic French reduction of vinegar, sugar and, usually, fruit—into this tart cocktail.

Ice
2 ounces brandy
¾ ounce Cointreau or other triple sec
½ ounce fresh lemon juice
½ ounce Vanilla-Cardamom Gastrique (below)

Fill a cocktail shaker with ice. Add all of the remaining ingredients and shake well. Strain into a chilled martini glass.

VANILLA-CARDAMOM GASTRIQUE
In a small saucepan, combine 1 cup sugar with 2 tablespoons water and ¼ teaspoon fresh lemon juice. Cook over moderately high heat until a golden brown caramel forms, 8 to 10 minutes; occasionally wash down the side of the pan with a wet pastry brush. Off the heat, carefully stir in 6 tablespoons cider vinegar. Add ½ vanilla bean and 5 crushed cardamom pods and let steep for 20 minutes. Strain into an airtight container and let cool completely, then refrigerate for up to 2 weeks. Makes about 8 ounces.

accoutrement

ARNAUD'S FRENCH 75 BAR,
NEW ORLEANS

Obsessed with Strega, a
saffron-scented, bright yellow
Italian liqueur, Chris Hannah
creates cocktails with it
whenever he can. This spicy
drink is his latest effort.

Ice

2 ounces Calvados
¾ ounce Strega
½ ounce Créole Shrubb or
  Grand Marnier
¾ ounce fresh lemon juice
2 dashes of Peychaud's bitters
3 brandied cherries

Fill a cocktail shaker with ice. Add
all of the remaining ingredients
except the cherries and shake well.
Strain into a chilled martini glass;
garnish with the cherries.

grandfather

SONA,
LOS ANGELES

Bartender Sam Ross prepares
this drink with Laird's bonded
(100 proof) apple brandy
because of the spirit's intense
flavor. Twenty pounds of
Virginia apples go into each
750-milliliter bottle.

Ice

1 ounce apple brandy,
  preferably bonded
1 ounce bourbon
1 ounce Carpano Antica Formula
  or other sweet vermouth
Dash of Angostura bitters
Dash of Peychaud's bitters
3 brandied cherries

Fill a pint glass with ice. Add all
of the remaining ingredients
except the cherries; stir well.
Strain into a chilled coupe and
garnish with the cherries.

brandy

northern spy

THE ALEMBIC,
SAN FRANCISCO

Bartender Josey Packard makes her own apricot brandy for this cocktail by infusing Cognac with dried fruit.

Ice
2 ounces apple brandy, preferably bonded
1½ ounces apple cider
½ ounce fresh lemon juice
¼ ounce apricot brandy
1 thin apple slice

Fill a cocktail shaker with ice. Add all of the remaining ingredients except the apple slice and shake well. Strain into a chilled coupe and garnish with the apple slice.

pink lady

TEARDROP
COCKTAIL LOUNGE,
PORTLAND, OR

TearDrop's bartenders adhere to the classic Pink Lady recipe for this brandy drink, which they tint with homemade grenadine.

1½ ounces gin
¾ ounce apple brandy, preferably bonded
¾ ounce fresh lemon juice
¾ ounce grenadine, preferably homemade (p. 14)
1 large egg white
Ice

Fill a cocktail shaker with all of the ingredients except the ice; shake well for 10 seconds. Add ice and shake again. Strain into a chilled coupe.

harvest sling

PDT,
MANHATTAN

The late Ngiam Tong Boon of Raffles Hotel in Singapore, who's credited with inventing the Singapore Sling around 1915, might be flattered by beverage director John Deragon's fall fruit–based update of the classic tropical cooler.

Ice

1½ ounces apple brandy, preferably bonded

¾ ounce sweet vermouth

¾ ounce fresh lemon juice

½ ounce Bénédictine (brandy-based herbal liqueur)

½ ounce Cherry Heering or other cherry liqueur

1½ ounces chilled ginger beer

1 brandied cherry and

¼ orange wheel

Fill a cocktail shaker with ice. Add all of the remaining ingredients except the ginger beer, cherry and orange wheel and shake well. Strain into an ice-filled collins glass. Stir in the ginger beer and garnish with the brandied cherry and the orange wheel quarter.

apricot sour

CENTRAL MICHEL RICHARD,
WASHINGTON, DC

The inventive cocktails at Central, Michel Richard's casual alternative to his flagship Citronelle, mirror the restaurant's updated American dishes, such as lobster burgers and crab cakes with leek tartar sauce.

1½ ounces apricot brandy
1 ounce sweet vermouth
1 ounce fresh lemon juice
1 large egg
3 dashes of orange bitters
Ice
1 fresh apricot slice skewered on a pick with 1 brandied cherry

Put the brandy, vermouth, lemon juice, egg and bitters in a cocktail shaker and shake well for 10 seconds. Add ice and shake again. Strain into an ice-filled rocks glass. Garnish with the apricot slice and cherry.

vermouth sin nombre

ALÓ,
DALLAS

Beverage director Ivan Rimach, who nicknamed this drink the Peruvian Manhattan, uses the Peruvian brandy pisco as a nod to Aló's South American menu.

½ lime, quartered
1¼ orange wheels
¾ ounce Simple Syrup (p. 14)
Ice cubes, plus crushed ice
2 ounces pisco
1 ounce sweet vermouth
1 ounce fresh orange juice

In a cocktail shaker, muddle the lime with 1 orange wheel and the Simple Syrup. Add ice cubes and the pisco, vermouth and orange juice; shake well. Strain into a crushed ice–filled rocks glass. Garnish with the orange wheel quarter.

APRICOT SOUR

"Freddie" tumbler by William Yeoward; sterling martini pick from TableArt.

CAFFÈ DI ALPI, P. 149
FRASCA FOOD & WINE,
BOULDER, CO
*"Bistro" double-wall glass
from Bodum.*

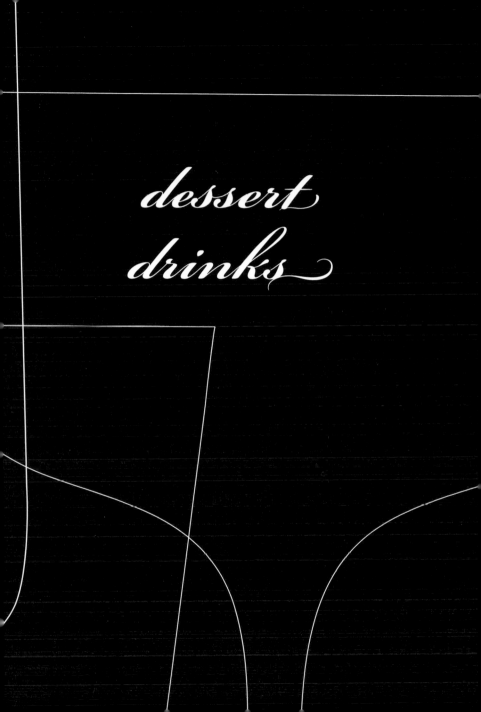

dessert

drinks

dessert drinks

mayan mocha martini

WEST END TAVERN,
BOULDER, CO

Beverage director James Lee uses tequila, Mexican coffee liqueur and crème de cacao to evoke the flavors of two Mexican specialties: Ibarra chocolate and *café de olla,* a traditional spiced coffee.

Ice
1½ ounces blanco tequila
½ ounce coffee liqueur
½ ounce dark crème de cacao
¾ ounce half-and-half
Pinch each of ground cinnamon
    and cayenne pepper

Fill a cocktail shaker with ice. Add the tequila, coffee liqueur, crème de cacao and half-and-half and shake well. Strain into a chilled martini glass and garnish with the cinnamon and cayenne.

off kilter

ELIXIR,
SAN FRANCISCO

Elixir owner H. Joseph Ehrmann was sharing drinks one night with Scotch whisky expert Steve Beal, when Beal asked him to create a cocktail pairing walnut liqueur and Johnnie Walker Gold. Off Kilter is the happy result.

Ice
2 ounces single-malt Scotch
½ ounce Grand Marnier
¼ ounce nocino (walnut liqueur)
½ ounce heavy cream
Pinch each of freshly grated nutmeg
    and freshly ground pepper

Fill a cocktail shaker with ice. Add the Scotch, Grand Marnier, nocino and cream and shake well. Strain into a snifter and garnish with the nutmeg and pepper.

chocolate-cherry margarita

LOS DADOS,
MANHATTAN

On a tucked-away corner in Manhattan's meatpacking district, Los Dados chef Sue Torres serves up homey Mexican food and excellent sangria and margaritas. She created this chocolate-accented cherry margarita to celebrate New Year's Eve 2007.

1 lime wedge and cocoa sugar (a mixture of 1 teaspoon each of unsweetened cocoa powder and vanilla sugar and a pinch of kosher salt)

5 brandied cherries

¾ ounce fresh lime juice

Ice

1½ ounces reposado tequila

¾ ounce Cointreau or other triple sec

Moisten half of the outer rim of a martini glass with the lime wedge and coat lightly with cocoa sugar. In a cocktail shaker, muddle the brandied cherries with the lime juice. Add ice and the tequila and Cointreau and shake well. Strain into the prepared martini glass.

dessert drinks

the hirshfield

PIN-UP BOWL,
ST. LOUIS

This bar and bowling alley partners serious, classically prepared cocktails with fun, light-hearted drinks like this homage to Leo Hirshfield, creator of the Tootsie Roll, one of America's first penny candies.

1 orange wedge and unsweetened cocoa powder

Ice

2 ounces chocolate vodka
½ ounce vanilla vodka
½ ounce dark crème de cacao
¼ ounce Grand Marnier
1 orange twist

Moisten half of the outer rim of a martini glass with the orange wedge and coat lightly with cocoa powder. Fill a cocktail shaker with ice. Add all of the remaining ingredients except the twist and shake well. Strain into the prepared martini glass and garnish with the orange twist.

stinger

THE BOAT HOUSE,
LAMBERTVILLE, NJ

The Stinger was likely inspired by Harry Johnson's 1882 *New and Improved Bartenders' Manual*. It combines that book's recipes for Brandy and Mint with Crème de Menthe.

Ice cubes, plus crushed ice

2 ounces Cognac
¾ ounce white crème de menthe
1 mint sprig

Fill a cocktail shaker with ice. Add the Cognac and crème de menthe and shake well. Strain into a crushed ice–filled rocks glass and garnish with the mint sprig.

THE HIRSHFIELD
"Vitis" martini glass by Riedel.

babylon sister

ABSINTHE BRASSERIE & BAR,
SAN FRANCISCO

Both this cocktail's name and its ingredients allude to one of bar manager Jonny Raglin's favorite Steely Dan tunes, "Babylon Sisters," which includes the line "drink kirschwasser from a shell."

1 lemon wedge and unsweetened cocoa powder

Ice

1 ounce kirsch (cherry eau-de-vie)

½ ounce maraschino liqueur

¼ ounce white crème de cacao

½ ounce heavy cream

¼ ounce Simple Syrup (p. 14)

3 brandied cherries skewered on a pick

Moisten half of the outer rim of a martini glass with the lemon wedge and coat lightly with cocoa powder. Fill a cocktail shaker with ice. Add all of the remaining ingredients except the cherries and shake well. Strain into the prepared martini glass and garnish with the skewered cherries.

chai almond deluxe

LE BAR AT SOFITEL, CHICAGO

Drink consultant Chad Solomon was inspired to create the Chai Almond Deluxe while reading *Shantaram*, a novel set in Mumbai.

2 ounces Chai-Infused Cognac (below)
½ ounce Honey Syrup (p. 49)
1½ ounces vanilla almond milk
½ teaspoon pure vanilla extract
1 large egg white
Ice

In a cocktail shaker, combine all of the ingredients except the ice and shake for 10 seconds. Add ice and shake again. Strain into a chilled coupe.

CHAI-INFUSED COGNAC In a jar, combine 8 ounces Cognac with 2 chai tea bags. Let stand for 2 hours. Strain into an airtight container and refrigerate for up to 1 week. Makes 8 ounces.

dessert drinks

the duchess

PROOF,
WASHINGTON, DC

Wine director Sebastian Zutant believes drinks have personalities. Because this cocktail is rich and elegant, he dubbed it The Duchess. "It's round and supple," he says, but the limoncello still packs a punch: "I want my drinks to taste like drinks."

½   ounce limoncello
1½ ounces vanilla vodka
2   ounces unsweetened coconut milk
1   large egg white
¼   ounce Simple Syrup (p. 14)
½   ounce fresh lemon juice
Ice

In a cocktail shaker, combine all of the ingredients except the ice and shake for 10 seconds. Add ice and shake again. Strain the drink into a chilled coupe.

absinthe suisse

LÜKE,
NEW ORLEANS

Widely available in 19th-century New Orleans saloons, fine French and Swiss absinthes were key to drinks like this one, loosely based on the Suissesse Cocktail in Stanley Clisby Arthur's *Famous New Orleans Drinks and How to Mix 'Em* from 1937.

1½ ounces Herbsaint or absinthe
¼   ounce Simple Syrup (p. 14)
3   ounces half-and-half
Dash of orange flower water
1   large egg white
¼   ounce white crème de menthe
Ice

In a cocktail shaker, combine all of the ingredients except the ice and shake for 10 seconds. Add ice and shake again. Strain into an ice-filled highball glass.

dessert drinks

café crème

ENOTECA SAN MARCO,
LAS VEGAS

In Italy, espresso spiked with Sambuca is called *caffè corretto* (which literally means "corrected coffee"). Bar manager Adam Wilson adds a few more ingredients to his version.

Ice
1 ounce Irish Cream
¾ ounce Sambuca
¾ ounce Frangelico
2 ounces whole milk
Pinch of ground coffee

Fill a cocktail shaker with ice. Add all of the remaining ingredients except the coffee and shake well. Strain into a chilled martini glass and garnish with the ground coffee.

caffè di alpi

FRASCA FOOD & WINE,
BOULDER, CO

Bartender Steve Peters dreamed up Caffè di Alpi ("Alpine Coffee" in Italian) as a deliciously warming après-ski drink.

1 teaspoon honey
3 ounces hot brewed coffee
1½ ounces bourbon
1 large dollop of Alps Whipped Cream (below)
Pinch of freshly grated nutmeg

Put the honey in a warmed mug. Add the hot coffee and the bourbon and stir. Top with Alps Whipped Cream and garnish with the grated nutmeg.

ALPS WHIPPED CREAM In a small bowl, beat 4 ounces heavy cream until thickened. Add ¾ ounce *amaro* (bittersweet Italian liqueur) and beat until firm. Makes enough whipped cream to top 3 drinks.

TANTE'S MEDICINE
"Mami" snifter by Alessi.

dessert drinks

tante's medicine

**ROUX,
PORTLAND, OR**

At the time she was preparing her bar menu, mixologist Molly Finnegan felt under the weather and uninspired. After a 2 a.m. brainstorming session, this sensational hot toddy improved both her cold and her drink list.

5 ounces hot brewed Earl Grey tea
2 ounces B&B Liqueur
¼ ounce fresh lemon juice
¼ ounce fresh orange juice
½ teaspoon honey
Ground cinnamon, freshly grated
    nutmeg and 1 cinnamon stick

In a snifter, stir the tea with the B&B, lemon and orange juices and the honey. Garnish with the ground cinnamon, grated nutmeg and the cinnamon stick.

hot toddy

**MIMS BRASSERIE,
PORTLAND, ME**

Along with soothing drinks like this toddy, Mims serves up hearty French dishes like mussels with bacon and Calvados, rabbit cassoulet with veal sausage and lobster bouillabaisse.

¼ ounce honey
6 ounces hot brewed
    lemon-ginger tea
1½ ounces Irish whiskey
½ ounce fresh orange juice
1 orange twist

Put the honey in a warmed mug. Add the hot tea and stir to dissolve the honey. Stir in the Irish whiskey and orange juice and garnish with the orange twist.

BLACKBERRY & CABERNET
CAIPIRINHA, P. 161
CANTINA,
SAN FRANCISCO
Wineglass by
Mario Cioni
from Takashimaya;
"Pulse" pitcher
by Calvin Klein.

pitcher drinks

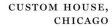

pitcher drinks

notre vermouth

**CUSTOM HOUSE,
CHICAGO**

With the aid of a pocket
French dictionary, bar
manager Timothy Lacey
managed to translate this
recipe from a book of
wine-based cocktails entitled
Vins Apéritifs Maison.

MAKES 6 DRINKS

Finely grated zest of 2 small oranges
2 chamomile tea bags
1 bottle (750 ml) Sauvignon Blanc
4 ounces vodka
¼ cup sugar
8 cinnamon sticks
Ice

In an airtight container, combine
the orange zest, tea bags,
Sauvignon Blanc, vodka, sugar
and 2 of the cinnamon sticks.
Refrigerate for 2 days, stirring
occasionally. Pour through a fine
strainer into a pitcher, then pour
the drink into ice-filled white
wine glasses. Garnish each drink
with a cinnamon stick.

de la costa bloody mary

DE LA COSTA,
CHICAGO

Drink consultant Jamie Terrell's recipe for the house Bloody Mary, inspired by the classic Bullshot, incorporates the tangy South American condiment chimichurri along with veal stock and freshly pressed tomato water.

MAKES 6 DRINKS

3 ounces vodka
18 ounces tomato juice
6 ounces veal or beef stock
3 ounces fresh lemon juice
1 tablespoon Worcestershire sauce
1½ teaspoons prepared chimichurri sauce
¾ teaspoon prepared horseradish cream
1 teaspoon Tabasco
1 lemon wedge and celery salt
(a mixture of 1 teaspoon each of celery salt, kosher salt and freshly ground pepper)
Ice
Freshly grated horseradish (optional)
6 cherry tomatoes

1. In a pitcher, combine the vodka, tomato juice, stock, lemon juice, Worcestershire sauce, chimichurri, horseradish cream and Tabasco; refrigerate the Bloody Mary mix until chilled, at least 1 hour.

2. Moisten half of the outer rims of 6 collins glasses with the lemon wedge and coat lightly with the celery salt mixture. Fill the glasses with ice. Stir the Bloody Mary mix and strain it into the prepared glasses. Grate fresh horseradish over each drink and garnish with the cherry tomatoes.

shinsei sangria

SHINSEI,
DALLAS

In keeping with the restaurant's Asian menu, Shinsei bartenders stir lychees and sake into their house white sangria.

MAKES 6 DRINKS

1 pear, sliced
1 orange, sliced
2 Granny Smith apples, sliced
8 canned lychees, drained
½ pineapple, peeled and cut into large chunks
8 ounces vodka
8 ounces Sauvignon Blanc
8 ounces sake
Ice

In an airtight container, combine all of the ingredients except the ice and refrigerate for at least 24 hours. Strain the mixture into a pitcher, discarding all the fruit except 6 of the lychees. Pour the sangria into ice-filled white wine glasses and garnish with the reserved lychees.

SHINSEI SANGRIA
"Wisteria" pitcher
by William Yeoward.

granada de amor

ANDINA,
PORTLAND, OR

The aromatic damiana plant, which grows throughout Mexico and is used to make Damiana liqueur, was thought to be an aphrodisiac by the Guaycura Indians, who inhabited Baja California until the late 1700s.

MAKES 6 DRINKS

12 ounces citrus vodka

3 ounces Damiana (Mexican herbal liqueur)

4½ ounces fresh lime juice

4½ ounces fresh orange juice

1½ ounces Cinnamon Syrup (below)

6 orange twists

In a pitcher, combine all of the ingredients except the twists and refrigerate until chilled, at least 1 hour. Stir and strain into chilled martini glasses. Garnish with the orange twists.

CINNAMON SYRUP In a heatproof bowl, combine 6 ounces hot Simple Syrup (p. 14) with four 3-inch cinnamon sticks. Let cool, then refrigerate overnight. Strain the syrup into an airtight container and refrigerate for up to 2 weeks. Makes 6 ounces.

capetown collins

NO. 9 PARK,
BOSTON

This cocktail gets its spicy, slightly nutty flavor from rooibos, a South African shrub used to make tea.

MAKES 6 DRINKS

- 12 ounces gin
- 12 ounces Rosemary-Rooibos Syrup (below)
- 9 ounces fresh lemon juice
- Ice
- 6 rosemary sprigs

In a pitcher, combine the gin, Rosemary-Rooibos Syrup and lemon juice and refrigerate until chilled, at least 1 hour. Stir well and strain into ice-filled collins glasses. Garnish with the rosemary sprigs.

ROSEMARY-ROOIBOS SYRUP
In a small saucepan, bring 2 cups water to a boil with 1 rosemary sprig; simmer over moderate heat for 5 minutes. Remove from the heat. Add 2 rooibos tea bags and let steep for 5 minutes. Discard the tea bags and rosemary and stir in 1 cup superfine sugar until dissolved. Let cool, then pour into an airtight container and refrigerate for up to 2 weeks. Makes about 14 ounces.

pitcher drinks

pimm's iced tea cup

BEMELMANS BAR,
MANHATTAN

Consulting mixologist Brian Van Flandern created this summery Pimm's Cup with country club cocktails in mind. "The key," says Van Flandern, "is to steep the mint tea for only one minute to avoid bitterness."

MAKES 6 DRINKS

- 6 ounces Pimm's No. 1 (English gin-based aperitif)
- 3 ounces gin
- 12 ounces chilled brewed mint tea
- 3 ounces Ginger Syrup (below)
- 3 ounces fresh lemon juice
- ¼ teaspoon orange bitters
- 12 ounces chilled ginger beer

Ice
- 6 unpeeled cucumber wheels, 6 orange wheel quarters and 6 mint sprigs

In a pitcher, combine the Pimm's, gin, mint tea, Ginger Syrup, lemon juice and orange bitters and refrigerate until chilled, at least 1 hour. Add the ginger beer to the pitcher, stir and strain the drink into ice-filled collins glasses. Garnish with the cucumber wheels, orange wheel quarters and mint sprigs.

GINGER SYRUP In a heatproof bowl, combine 6 ounces hot Simple Syrup (p. 14) and 1 tablespoon chopped fresh ginger. Let cool, then refrigerate overnight. Strain the syrup into an airtight container and refrigerate for up to 2 weeks. Makes about 6 ounces.

blackberry & cabernet caipirinha

**CANTINA,
SAN FRANCISCO**

For this punch-like take on the caipirinha, Cantina uses a Cabernet blended with a good amount of spicy Syrah.

MAKES 6 DRINKS

24	blackberries
4	ounces Simple Syrup (p. 14)
12	ounces cachaça (potent Brazilian sugarcane spirit)
4	ounces Cabernet Sauvignon
8	ounces fresh orange juice
2	ounces fresh lime juice
Ice	
6	lime wheels and 6 orange wheels

In a pitcher, muddle 12 of the blackberries with the Simple Syrup. Add the cachaça, Cabernet and the orange and lime juices and refrigerate until chilled, at least 1 hour. Stir well and strain the drink into ice-filled white wine glasses. Garnish with the remaining 12 blackberries and the lime and orange wheels.

KILL-DEVIL PUNCH
*"Frosted Band" glasses
by Calvin Klein;
"Trudy" bowl by
William Yeoward.*

kill-devil punch

**DEATH & CO.,
MANHATTAN**

Death & Co. co-owner
David Kaplan spent months
bidding on the vintage
bowls and cups in which he
now serves punches.

MAKES 6 DRINKS

9 ounces amber rum
6 ounces pineapple juice
5 ounces Simple Syrup (p. 14)
4 ounces fresh lime juice
Raspberry Ice (below)
5 ounces chilled Champagne
12 raspberries and 12 lime wheels

In a pitcher, combine the rum,
pineapple juice, Simple Syrup
and lime juice and refrigerate
until chilled, at least 1 hour.
Stir and strain into a punch bowl.
Add the Raspberry Ice. Pour
in the Champagne and stir once.
Garnish with the raspberries
and lime wheels. Serve in small
rocks glasses or tea cups.

RASPBERRY ICE Pour 12 ounces
water into a wide, shallow
plastic container and arrange
24 raspberries in the water.
Freeze for at least 6 hours. Set
the bottom of the mold in a
bowl of hot water to release the
ice. Makes one 12-ounce block
of Raspberry Ice.

pitcher drinks

boston tea party

KO PRIME,
BOSTON

Cocktail consultant Jacques
Bezuidenhout created
this classic five-ingredient
punch, which is
served in tea cups.

MAKES 6 DRINKS

9 ounces aged *rhum agricole*
(aromatic West Indian rum)

1½ ounces Créole Shrubb or
Grand Marnier

12 ounces chilled brewed chai

1½ ounces fresh lime juice

6 orange twists, curled
into spirals

In a pitcher, combine the *rhum agricole,* Créole Shrubb, brewed chai and lime juice and refrigerate until chilled, at least 1 hour. Stir and strain into chilled tea cups. Garnish the drinks with the curled orange twists.

presbyterian

**ZEPPELIN,
MANHATTAN**

The original Presbyterian was probably a mocktail, suitable for abstemious churchgoers, that combined ginger ale and club soda to look like a highball (minus the whiskey). Zeppelin owners Jason Kosmas and Dushan Zaric spice up the recipe with a savory house-made ginger beer.

MAKES 6 DRINKS

12 ounces rye whiskey
6   ounces Ginger-Mint Syrup (below)
4½ ounces fresh lime juice
18 thin lime wheels
Ice
12 ounces chilled club soda
6   mint sprigs

In a pitcher, combine the rye, Ginger-Mint Syrup and lime juice; refrigerate until chilled, at least 1 hour. Press 3 lime wheels on the inside of each of 6 collins glasses and fill with ice. Stir the club soda into the pitcher, then pour into the prepared glasses. Garnish with the mint.

GINGER-MINT SYRUP Peel and chop ¾ pound fresh ginger and 1 cucumber, then finely chop in a food processor with 1 cup fresh mint. Transfer to a saucepan. Add 2 cups turbinado sugar, ¾ cup honey, 16 ounces water, 4 ounces fresh lime juice and 1 teaspoon black peppercorns; simmer over moderate heat for 10 minutes. Strain into a bowl, pressing on the solids. Wipe out the pan. Pour in the mixture and simmer over low heat until thick enough to coat a spoon, 10 minutes. Let cool; refrigerate in an airtight container for up to 2 weeks. Makes about 17 ounces.

figa

CLYDE COMMON,
PORTLAND, OR

Figa was bar manager Charlie Hodge's first cocktail on the drink list at Clyde Common, which opened in 2007 in Portland's retro-minimalist Ace Hotel.

MAKES 6 DRINKS

12 ounces Fig Vodka (below)
6 ounces chilled brewed
   Earl Grey tea
9 ounces fresh tangerine juice
Ice
6 fresh fig wedges

In a pitcher, combine all of the ingredients except the ice and fig wedges and refrigerate until chilled, at least 1 hour. Stir well. Strain into ice-filled highball glasses and garnish with the fresh fig wedges.

FIG VODKA In a jar, combine 24 ounces vodka and 12 dried figs. Cover and refrigerate for 2 days. Strain the vodka into an airtight container and refrigerate for up to 3 weeks. Makes 24 ounces.

FIGA

"Curtain Call" highball glass by Barbara Barry for Wedgwood; "Branch" spoon by Blue Leaves from Tabula Tua.

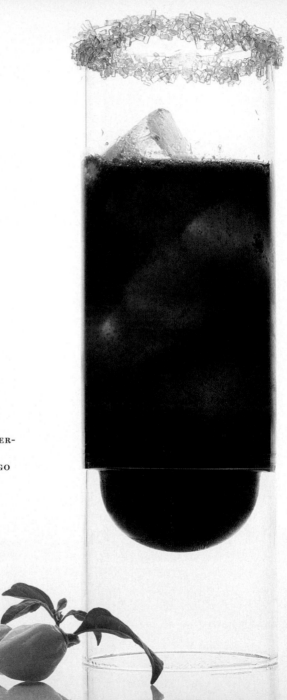

POMEGRANATE-GINGER-
CHILE NOJITO, P. 171
NACIONAL 27, CHICAGO
"Float" glass by Molo.

mocktails

mocktails

tall cool one

**CANLIS,
SEATTLE**

This mocktail was inspired by head bartender Laren Waterbury's favorite summer cocktail *with* alcohol, the Chill 'em (gin, grapefruit juice, orange bitters and tonic), which he created while bartending in Houston during an August heat wave.

Ice

1½ ounces fresh grapefruit juice
¾ ounce Juniper Tea Syrup (below)
¾ ounce fresh lime juice
2 ounces chilled tonic water
1 grapefruit twist

Fill a cocktail shaker with ice. Add the grapefruit juice, Juniper Tea Syrup and lime juice and shake well. Strain into an ice-filled highball glass, stir in the tonic and garnish with the grapefruit twist.

JUNIPER TEA SYRUP In a heatproof bowl, combine 9 ounces hot Simple Syrup (p. 14) with 2 Earl Grey tea bags and let steep for 5 minutes. Discard the tea bags and add 6 crushed juniper berries. Let cool, then strain into an airtight container and refrigerate for up to 2 weeks. Makes 9 ounces.

pomegranate-ginger-chile nojito

NACIONAL 27, CHICAGO

All of Nacional 27's cocktails are collaborations with the kitchen. This one took shape after mixologist Adam Seger tasted an amazing mango-habanero salad dressing.

2 ounces pomegranate juice and coarse sugar

Ice

½ lime, quartered

8 mint leaves

¾ ounce Ginger-Habanero Syrup (below)

3 ounces chilled club soda

Moisten the outer rim of a collins glass with 1 ounce of the pomegranate juice and coat lightly with sugar. Fill the glass with ice. In a cocktail shaker, muddle the lime quarters with the mint leaves and Ginger-Habanero Syrup. Add ice and the remaining 1 ounce of pomegranate juice and shake well. Strain into the prepared collins glass and stir in the club soda.

GINGER-HABANERO SYRUP
In a heatproof bowl, combine 6 ounces hot Simple Syrup (p. 14) with 1 tablespoon plus 1 teaspoon chopped fresh ginger and 1 halved and seeded habanero chile; let steep for 10 minutes. Strain into an airtight container and let cool completely. Refrigerate for up to 2 weeks. Makes 6 ounces.

mocktails

strawberry & ginger cooler

ABSINTHE BRASSERIE & BAR, SAN FRANCISCO

At the Belle Epoque–style Absinthe Brasserie, general manager and cocktail book author Jeff Hollinger serves up modern adaptations of 19th-century classic drinks. His Strawberry & Ginger Cooler is one of the few nonalcoholic refreshers on the menu.

2 large strawberries, sliced, plus
1 strawberry half
½-inch piece of fresh ginger, chopped
½ ounce Simple Syrup (p. 14)
Ice
2 ounces fresh orange juice
1 ounce fresh lime juice
2 ounces chilled ginger beer

In a cocktail shaker, muddle the strawberry slices with the chopped ginger and Simple Syrup. Add ice and the orange and lime juices and shake well. Double strain (p. 17) into an ice-filled collins glass. Stir in the ginger beer and garnish with the strawberry half.

STRAWBERRY & GINGER COOLER

"Mimosa" flute from Crate & Barrel; "Drops" vase by Renzo Stellon for Salviati.

mocktails

thé glacé

COCOLIQUOT,
MADISON, WI

Thé Glacé ("Iced Tea" in French) is a nonalcoholic variation on a house cocktail made with framboise, tea and lemon soda.

Ice
2 teaspoons raspberry preserves
¾ ounce fresh lemon juice
6 ounces chilled brewed
   Ceylon black tea
½ ounce Simple Syrup (p. 14)
1 lemon wedge

Fill a cocktail shaker with ice. Add the raspberry preserves, lemon juice, tea and Simple Syrup and shake well. Double strain (p. 17) into an ice-filled collins glass and garnish with the lemon wedge.

coral reef

TRADER VIC'S,
DALLAS

Sven Koch, former head bartender at Trader Vic's in Düsseldorf, Germany, won a contest in 1994 for his Coral Reef—competing against "real" cocktails. It was soon added to Trader Vic's master cocktail menu.

1 ounce unsweetened coconut milk
1 ounce mango nectar
4 whole strawberries
3 ounces pineapple juice
1 cup ice cubes
1 pineapple spear and 1 mint sprig

In a blender, combine all of the ingredients except the pineapple spear and mint sprig and puree. Pour into into a red wine glass and garnish with the pineapple spear and mint sprig.

lady lavender's mocktail

RESTAURANT EUGENE, ATLANTA

This drink was mixologist Gregory Best's response to a woman dressed in lavender who tottered into Restaurant Eugene with friends for a nightcap. "My darling," she said, "one more will put me directly over the edge. Fruit juice, please."

Ice

- 3 ounces fresh grapefruit juice
- ¾ ounce Lavender Syrup (below)
- ¼ ounce grenadine, preferably homemade (p. 14)
- 2 ounces chilled club soda
- 1 basil sprig
- 1 fresh lavender sprig (optional)

Fill a cocktail shaker with ice. Add the grapefruit juice, Lavender Syrup and grenadine and shake well. Strain into an ice-filled collins glass, stir in the club soda and garnish with the basil and lavender sprigs.

LAVENDER SYRUP In a heatproof bowl, combine 6 ounces hot Simple Syrup (p. 14) with ½ teaspoon dried lavender buds. Let stand for 25 minutes, then strain into an airtight container and let cool completely. Refrigerate for up to 2 weeks. Makes about 6 ounces.

SOPHISTICATED LADY (LEFT)
"Flora" cocktail glass by Johann Grawunder for Salviati.

FUJI APPLE SODA
"Tao Garden" glass by Kenzo.

sophisticated lady

EASTERN STANDARD,
BOSTON

Bar manager Jackson Cannon wanted to serve a mocktail that was neither soda-driven nor a supersweet "juice bomb." The result: this savory take on a cosmopolitan.

1   unpeeled cucumber wheel, plus
    1 peeled cucumber spear
1   ounce Simple Syrup (p. 14)
¼   teaspoon salt
Ice
2   ounces cranberry juice
1   ounce fresh lime juice

In a cocktail shaker, muddle the cucumber wheel, Simple Syrup and salt. Add ice and the juices and shake well. Double strain (p. 17) into a chilled martini glass. Garnish with the spear.

fuji apple soda

BACKSTREET CAFÉ,
HOUSTON

As soon as beverage director Sean Beck spotted a new line of apple-flavored juices and sodas at a grocery store, he decided to make one of his own. After a spirited discussion of apples with a winemaker, Beck chose the Fuji as the base for his drink.

Ice
2   ounces Apple-Ginger Syrup (below)
3   ounces chilled club soda
2   apple slices

Fill a highball glass with ice. Add the Apple-Ginger Syrup and soda; stir. Garnish with the apple slices.

APPLE-GINGER SYRUP In a jar, combine 16 ounces apple juice (preferably Fuji) with ⅓ cup honey and 1 tablespoon plus 1 teaspoon chopped fresh ginger; refrigerate overnight. Strain into an airtight container and add 5 ounces cranberry juice. Refrigerate for up to 1 week. Makes about 22 ounces.

JICAMA-MANGO GUACAMOLE, P. 182
MERCADITO CANTINA, MANHATTAN
"Pizzicati" bowl by
Norbetto Moretti for Salviati.

bar food

MARINATED OLIVES
"Float" martini glass by Molo.

marinated olives

GEORGE'S AT THE COVE,
SAN DIEGO

These spicy olives are always on the menu at George's recently renovated bar; they're infused with fennel, a favorite flavoring of chef Trey Foshee. "The licorice flavor always makes me hungry," he says.

MAKES 2 POUNDS

1   tablespoon fennel seeds
1   pound Niçoise olives (2½ cups)
1   pound Picholine olives (2½ cups)
5   large garlic cloves, crushed
1   tablespoon crushed red pepper
Zest strips from 1 orange, cut into
    fine julienne
About 1 cup extra-virgin olive oil

1. In a small skillet, toast the fennel seeds over moderate heat until fragrant, about 2 minutes.

2. Rinse the olives in a large strainer; drain well. Transfer the olives to a medium bowl. Stir in the toasted fennel seeds, garlic, crushed red pepper and orange zest and add enough olive oil to cover. Let stand at room temperature for at least 4 hours before serving.

MAKE AHEAD The olives can be refrigerated for up to 10 days. Bring to room temperature before serving.

jicama-mango guacamole

MERCADITO CANTINA,
MANHATTAN

While traveling through Mexico, chef Patricio Sandoval discovered the ubiquitous snack of thinly sliced mango and jicama spiked with lime and chile. Sandoval used the dish as inspiration for this guacamole, one of the most popular of several on the menu at Mercadito.

6 TO 8 SERVINGS

- 3   Hass avocados, cut into ½-inch dice
- 1   medium plum tomato, seeded and cut into ¼-inch dice
- ½   small onion, cut into ¼-inch dice
- ¾   cup finely diced ripe mango
- ½   cup finely diced peeled jicama
- 3   tablespoons finely chopped cilantro
- 1   medium chipotle in adobo, minced (1 tablespoon)
- 1   small jalapeño, seeded and minced
- 2   tablespoons fresh lemon juice

Kosher salt

Tortilla chips, for serving

In a large bowl, gently stir the avocados with the tomato, onion, mango, jicama, cilantro, chipotle, jalapeño and lemon juice until well mixed but still slightly chunky. Season with salt and serve with tortilla chips.

bar food

blue ribbon egg shooters

BLUE RIBBON DOWNING STREET BAR, MANHATTAN

Blue Ribbon's shooters don't involve downing raw eggs—rather, they're a spicy version of deviled eggs. The bar uses organic eggs from a farm in New York's Hudson Valley where 200 "pasture" chickens roam the grounds.

4 TO 6 SERVINGS

- 1 medium jalapeño
- 1 serrano chile
- 1 mild red chile, such as Holland
- 1 cup distilled white vinegar
- 6 large eggs
- 2 tablespoons mayonnaise
- ¼ teaspoon Dijon mustard
- ¼ teaspoon red wine vinegar
- Salt and freshly ground pepper
- Paprika

1. In a medium saucepan of boiling salted water, blanch the 3 chiles until softened slightly, about 4 minutes. Drain and cool the chiles under running water; pat dry. Transfer to a medium bowl, cover with the white vinegar and refrigerate overnight.

2. In a medium saucepan of boiling water, cook the eggs for 13 minutes. Drain and rinse the eggs under cold water until cool. Peel the eggs and halve lengthwise.

3. Meanwhile, drain the chiles and pat dry, then seed and finely chop them. In a small bowl, mix the mayonnaise with the mustard and red wine vinegar and season with salt and pepper.

4. Top the eggs with dollops of the mayonnaise and the pickled chiles and paprika and serve.

curried rice krispies squares

THE VIOLET HOUR, CHICAGO

Chef Justin Large, who also works as a sous chef at the beloved wine bar Avec, created these ingenious and addictive squares, an Indian-spiced variation on the all-American classic.

MAKES ABOUT 6 DOZEN 1-INCH SQUARES

3 tablespoons unsalted butter, plus more for greasing the dish

One 10-ounce bag marshmallows

2 tablespoons mild Madras curry powder

½ cup salted roasted sunflower seeds

6 cups Rice Krispies

1. Butter a 9-by-13-inch baking dish. In a large saucepan, melt the 3 tablespoons of butter. Add the marshmallows and cook over very low heat, stirring with a wooden spoon, until completely melted, about 5 minutes. Stir in the curry powder. Remove from the heat and add the sunflower seeds and Rice Krispies; stir until completely coated.

2. Scrape the mixture into the prepared baking dish and, using buttered hands, press into an even layer. Let stand at room temperature until cooled and firm.

3. Invert the curried Rice Krispies onto a work surface. Using a sharp knife, trim the edges to form a neat rectangle, then cut into 1-inch squares and serve.

CURRIED RICE KRISPIES SQUARES
"Afro" bowl by Dinosaur Designs.

sunflower seed & rosemary crackers

ROCCA KITCHEN & BAR, BOSTON

Rocca's consulting pastry chef, Ruth-Anne Adams, and her husband, Tom Fosnot, the restaurant's chef, sampled many breads while traveling through Liguria, Italy. A simple, sunflower seed–flecked cracker from the town of Chiavari was their favorite, and back at Rocca, they re-created it as a snack.

MAKES ABOUT 2 DOZEN CRACKERS

- 2 cups all-purpose flour
- ¼ cup raw sunflower seeds
- ½ teaspoon minced rosemary
- ¼ teaspoon active dry yeast

Salt

- ½ cup warm water
- ¼ cup plus 2 teaspoons extra-virgin olive oil

1. In a large bowl, mix the flour with the sunflower seeds, rosemary, yeast and 1½ teaspoons of salt. Stir in the water and ¼ cup of the olive oil until a dough forms. Turn the dough out onto a work surface and knead until it becomes a smooth ball, about 5 minutes. Transfer the dough to a bowl, cover with plastic wrap and let stand for 2 hours.

2. Preheat the oven to 350°. Turn 2 large baking sheets upside down. Divide the dough in half. Set 1 half on a baking sheet and roll it out to a 9-by-15-inch rectangle about ¹⁄₁₆ inch thick. Trim the edges to make a neat rectangle. Using a sharp knife, cut the dough crosswise into 1-inch-wide strips. Drizzle the tops with 1 teaspoon of the oil and season with salt. Repeat with the remaining dough and oil.

3. Bake the crackers for about 28 minutes, until golden. Let cool completely before serving.

pimento cheese

**HOLEMAN & FINCH
PUBLIC HOUSE,
ATLANTA**

Chef Linton Hopkins uses locally grown pimientos (heart-shaped sweet red peppers), which he cans himself, in this luxurious spread, an old Southern favorite.

6 SERVINGS

- 3   medium red bell peppers
- 5   ounces sharp yellow cheddar cheese, coarsely shredded (2 cups)
- 4   ounces cream cheese (½ cup), softened
- ¼   cup mayonnaise
- 1   tablespoon juice from a jar of bread and butter pickles (optional)
- ¼   teaspoon Tabasco

Kosher salt and freshly ground pepper
Saltine crackers, for serving

1. Light a grill or preheat the broiler. Set the bell peppers over a hot fire or under the broiler and cook, turning, until charred all over. Transfer the bell peppers to a plate and let cool.

2. Peel the roasted peppers and discard the cores and seeds. Cut the peppers into ⅛-inch dice and pat dry with paper towels.

3. In a medium bowl, mix the diced peppers with the cheddar, cream cheese, mayonnaise, pickle juice and Tabasco and season with salt and pepper. Cover and refrigerate for at least 2 hours. Serve with crackers.

artichoke dip

FLATBUSH FARM,
BROOKLYN, NY

Flatbush Farm feels like a cross between a French bistro, an English pub and a Brooklyn neighborhood joint, and the bar menu includes corresponding comfort foods. One is this all-American, over-the-top, cheese-smothered dip.

8 SERVINGS

1 large jalapeño
Four 9-ounce boxes frozen artichokes—thawed, drained and coarsely chopped
¾ cup mayonnaise
¾ cup freshly grated Parmigiano-Reggiano cheese
1 garlic clove, minced
1 tablespoon fresh lemon juice
1 teaspoon finely grated lemon zest
1 teaspoon kosher salt
1 teaspoon Tabasco
2½ ounces sharp white cheddar cheese, shredded (1 cup)
Crackers or sliced baguette, for serving

1. Preheat the oven to 350°. Roast the jalapeño directly over a gas flame, turning, until charred all over. Let cool, then peel and seed the jalapeño and cut it into ¼-inch dice.

2. In a large bowl, mix the artichokes with the jalapeño, mayonnaise, Parmigiano, garlic, lemon juice, lemon zest, salt and Tabasco. Transfer the mixture to a 1-quart baking dish. Bake for about 15 minutes, or until hot.

3. Preheat the broiler. Sprinkle the shredded cheddar evenly over the hot dip. Broil for about 2 minutes, until browned in spots and bubbly. Serve hot or warm, with crackers.

french onion dip

EASTERN STANDARD,
BOSTON

Marco Suarez, chef at this well-liked Kenmore Square restaurant, learned to make this dip at one of his first jobs, in a deli. It's a best seller during and after Red Sox games, when fans come in from nearby Fenway Park.

6 TO 8 SERVINGS

- 2 tablespoons vegetable oil
- 3 large sweet onions (2½ pounds), halved and thinly sliced
- 6 ounces cream cheese (¾ cup), softened
- ¼ cup sour cream
- ¼ cup mayonnaise
- 1½ teaspoons Dijon mustard
- 1 teaspoon Worcestershire sauce
- ¾ teaspoon garlic powder
- ¼ teaspoon onion powder

Kosher salt and freshly ground pepper
Potato chips, for serving

1. In a large skillet, heat the oil. Add the onions and cook over moderately high heat, stirring occasionally, until they begin to soften, about 10 minutes. Reduce the heat to moderate and continue to cook until the onions are light golden and softened, about 30 minutes. Remove from the heat and let cool to room temperature.

2. In a medium bowl, mix the cream cheese, sour cream, mayonnaise, mustard, Worcestershire sauce, garlic powder and onion powder. Stir in the onions and season with salt and pepper. Serve with potato chips.

FRIED PICKLES WITH
SPICY MAYONNAISE
*"Gayane" bowls by Kenzo
from Unica Home.*

fried pickles with spicy mayonnaise

**BOROUGH FOOD & DRINK,
MANHATTAN**

Consulting chef Zak Pelaccio
grew up eating fried pickles in
Brooklyn Heights, New York.
He coats his extra-crisp version
in *panko* (Japanese bread
crumbs) and fries them in
schmaltz, or chicken fat, though
vegetable oil works well, too.

6 SERVINGS

½ cup mayonnaise
1 small garlic clove, minced
¼ teaspoon cayenne pepper
Kosher salt and freshly ground black pepper
Vegetable oil or rendered chicken fat
  (schmaltz), for deep-frying
1 cup *panko* (Japanese bread cumbs)
2 large eggs, lightly beaten
½ cup all-purpose flour
5 half-sour or dill pickles, quartered
  lengthwise

1. In a small bowl, mix the mayonnaise
with the garlic and cayenne and season
with salt and black pepper.

2. In a medium saucepan, heat
1½ inches of oil to 350°. In a food
processor, pulse the *panko* until finely
ground. Transfer the *panko*, beaten
eggs and flour to 3 shallow bowls.
Dust the pickle spears in the flour and
tap off the excess, then dip them in
the beaten egg, letting any excess drip
off. Dredge the pickles in the *panko*
to coat thoroughly.

3. Fry the pickles in 2 batches until
golden, about 4 minutes. Transfer to
paper towels to drain. Serve hot, with
the spicy mayonnaise.

bitter ballen

RESTO,
MANHATTAN

Although these delectable fried
meatballs originated in
the Netherlands, they're also
popular in Belgium—and at Resto,
a hip Belgian restaurant.

8 SERVINGS

¾ pound ground veal
¼ pound ground pork
2 garlic cloves, minced
1 large shallot, minced
2 teaspoons kosher salt
¼ teaspoon freshly grated nutmeg
1⅓ cups fine dry bread crumbs
¼ cup plus 1 tablespoon milk
1 large egg yolk plus 2 large beaten eggs
½ cup coarsely shredded Gruyère cheese
½ cup plus 3 tablespoons tapioca starch
Vegetable oil, for frying

1. In a large bowl, mix the veal with the pork, garlic, shallot, salt and nutmeg. Refrigerate for 1 hour. In a bowl, mix ⅓ cup of the bread crumbs and the milk; let stand for 10 minutes. Transfer to a food processor and work to a paste. Stir the paste, egg yolk and Gruyère into the veal mixture. Roll into 1-inch balls; refrigerate for at least 1 hour.

2. Put ½ cup of the tapioca starch, the beaten eggs and the remaining 1 cup of bread crumbs in 3 bowls. Stir the remaining 3 tablespoons of tapioca starch into the bread crumbs. Dust each meatball in the tapioca. Roll in the eggs, then in the bread crumbs.

3. In a saucepan, heat 1½ inches of oil to 350°. Fry the meatballs in batches until golden and cooked through, about 4 minutes. Drain on paper towels; serve.

soy-glazed chicken yakitori

FEARING'S,
DALLAS

Walking into a yakitori bar in Tokyo, chef Dean Fearing was startled by the thick grill smoke filling the room, then delighted by the delicious flavor of the skewered meats. "These chicken skewers are as close to the food from that grill as I can remember," he says.

4 SERVINGS

1 pound skinless, boneless chicken thighs, cut into 1-inch pieces

4 scallions, white and light green parts only, cut into 1-inch lengths

6 shiitake mushroom caps, quartered

½ cup soy sauce

¼ cup mirin

2 tablespoons *kecap manis* (sweet Indonesian soy sauce)

2 tablespoons sugar

1 tablespoon minced fresh ginger

1 tablespoon Sriracha chile sauce

1 teaspoon minced garlic

Vegetable oil, for brushing

1. Thread each of 8 metal skewers with 3 pieces of chicken and 3 pieces each of scallion and shiitake.

2. In a saucepan, combine the soy sauce, mirin, *kecap manis,* sugar, ginger, Sriracha and garlic; bring to a boil. Simmer over low heat, stirring, until slightly thickened, 8 minutes.

3. Light a grill or preheat a grill pan. Brush the skewers with oil and grill over high heat, turning, until nearly cooked through, about 5 minutes. Brush the skewers with the sauce and grill, turning, until the chicken is cooked through and nicely glazed, about 3 minutes longer. Serve at once.

ike's vietnamese fish sauce wings

POK POK,
PORTLAND, OR

Chef-owner Andy Ricker, who takes annual trips to Southeast Asia, first tried fish sauce wings at a roadside stand in Saigon seven years ago. He scribbled down his guess at the ingredients on a paper napkin, which he carried with him until Pok Pok opened.

6 SERVINGS

½ cup Asian fish sauce
½ cup superfine sugar
4 garlic cloves, 2 crushed and 2 minced
3 pounds chicken wings, split at the drumettes
2 tablespoons vegetable oil, plus more for frying
1 cup cornstarch
1 tablespoon chopped cilantro
1 tablespoon chopped mint

1. In a bowl, whisk the fish sauce, sugar and crushed garlic. Add the wings and toss to coat. Refrigerate for 3 hours, tossing the wings occasionally.

2. Heat the 2 tablespoons of oil in a small skillet. Add the minced garlic; cook over moderate heat until golden, 3 minutes. Drain on paper towels.

3. In a large pot, heat 2 inches of oil to 350°. Pat the wings dry on paper towels; reserve the marinade. Put the cornstarch in a shallow bowl, add the wings and turn to coat. Fry the wings in batches until golden and cooked through, about 10 minutes. Drain on paper towels and transfer to a bowl.

4. In a small saucepan, simmer the marinade over moderately high heat until syrupy, 5 minutes. Strain over the wings and toss. Top with the cilantro, mint and fried garlic and serve.

SPICY SHRIMP WITH GARLIC BUTTER
Vintage "Solbjerg" bowl by Nils Thorssen for
Royal Copenhagen from The End of History.

spicy shrimp
with garlic butter

CATALAN FOOD & WINE,
HOUSTON

Back when chef Chris Shepherd
and his wife, Rocio Gonzalez,
were dating, she used to fix him
these outrageously good Spanish
shrimp, which are served
in a chile-spiced garlic butter.

4 TO 6 SERVINGS

16 jumbo shrimp (1½ pounds),
   shelled and deveined
Kosher salt and freshly ground pepper
2 tablespoons extra-virgin olive oil
2 large garlic cloves, thinly sliced
½ cup dry white wine
2 tablespoons *sambal oelek* or
   other chile paste
1 stick (4 ounces) unsalted butter,
   cut into tablespoons
Crusty bread, for serving

Season the shrimp with salt and
pepper. In a very large skillet,
heat the olive oil until shimmering.
Add the shrimp and cook over
moderately high heat until lightly
browned, about 3 minutes. Add
the garlic and cook until fragrant,
about 1 minute. Add the wine and
sambal and bring to a simmer,
scraping up any browned bits on the
bottom of the pan. Reduce the heat
to moderately low and swirl in the
butter until melted and incorporated.
Remove from the heat and season
with salt and pepper. Transfer to
a bowl and serve with crusty bread.

bacon-wrapped hot dogs with avocado

CRIF DOGS,
MANHATTAN

This late-night hot dog spot is locally famous for its franks. This one, which goes by the name The Chihuahua, is wrapped in bacon and topped with sour cream and avocado. It's also available at the adjoining cocktail lounge, PDT.

6 SERVINGS

6 hot dogs
6 slices of bacon
2 tablespoons vegetable oil
6 hot dog buns, split and warmed
1 Hass avocado, cut into 12 slices
¼ cup plus 2 tablespoons sour cream
¼ cup plus 2 tablespoons spicy salsa

1. Pat the hot dogs and bacon dry with paper towels. Wrap each hot dog with a slice of bacon in a spiral; secure the bacon at each end with a toothpick.

2. In a large skillet, heat the vegetable oil until shimmering. Add the hot dogs and cook over moderate heat, turning, until the bacon is crisp, about 5 minutes. Transfer the hot dogs to paper towels to drain. Discard the toothpicks.

3. Tuck the hot dogs in the buns. Top with the sliced avocado, sour cream and salsa and serve.

dark & stormy ribs

PRESIDIO SOCIAL CLUB,
SAN FRANCISCO

The glaze on these spicy, tender ribs cleverly incorporates the major components of the classic Dark 'n Stormy cocktail: ginger beer and dark rum.

6 SERVINGS

- ¼ cup kosher salt
- 1½ teaspoons freshly ground black pepper
- 1 teaspoon crushed red pepper
- 2 tablespoons granulated sugar
- 2 racks baby back ribs (3½ pounds)
- 2 cups ginger beer (16 ounces)
- 1 cup dark rum
- ½ cup lightly packed dark brown sugar
- 2 tablespoons soy sauce

1. In a small bowl, mix the salt with the black pepper, crushed red pepper and granulated sugar. On a large rimmed baking sheet, rub the seasoned salt all over the ribs and let stand for 2 hours.

2. Preheat the oven to 300°. In a large roasting pan, mix the ginger beer with the rum, brown sugar and soy sauce. Add the ribs and cover the pan tightly with foil. Braise the ribs in the oven for 1½ hours, or until tender; turn the ribs halfway through cooking.

3. Light a grill or preheat the broiler. Transfer the ribs to a cutting board; reserve the cooking liquid. Cut the racks into individual ribs. Grill the ribs over moderately high heat or broil them, turning, until lightly charred on all sides, about 3 minutes. Dip the ribs in the reserved cooking liquid, transfer to a platter and serve.

barbecue sloppy joes

KETCHUP,
LOS ANGELES

In contrast to its mod white tables and neon-red lamps, Ketchup dishes up old-school diner food. Before serving this hearty sandwich, which is spiked with the restaurant's signature condiment, chef Christopher Tunnell ran it by his mom. "When she tasted it, she was proud," he says.

6 SERVINGS

¼ cup vegetable oil
1 medium onion, cut into ¼-inch dice
¾ pound ground sirloin
¾ pound ground chuck
1 large garlic clove, minced
2 medium tomatoes—halved, seeded and cut into ½-inch dice
1½ cups ketchup
¾ cup prepared barbecue sauce
¼ cup tomato paste
2 tablespoons cider vinegar
Salt and freshly ground pepper
6 hamburger buns, split and toasted
½ pound sharp cheddar cheese, sliced

1. In a large skillet, heat the oil. Add the onion and cook over moderately high heat until beginning to brown, about 6 minutes. Push the onion to one side of the skillet and add the ground sirloin and chuck. Cook, stirring, until browned, about 12 minutes. Add the garlic and cook until fragrant, 1 minute. Stir in the tomatoes, ketchup, barbecue sauce, tomato paste and vinegar. Simmer over moderately low heat, stirring, until the sauce is thick, 20 minutes. Season with salt and pepper.

2. Preheat the broiler. Set the bun bottoms on serving plates. Lay the cheese on the bun tops and broil until melted, about 1 minute. Spoon the Sloppy Joe mixture on the buns; serve.

mini burgers & crispy onion rings

STAND,
MANHATTAN

These little burgers, listed as a side dish at Stand, are about half the size of the restaurant's standard ones. Like their larger counterparts, the mini burgers are extra juicy because they're made with a mixture of meats, including ground chuck and short rib. The accompanying onion rings are unbelievably crispy, thanks to the club soda in the batter.

MAKES 6 MINI BURGERS

1   pound ground chuck
¼   pound boneless short rib, minced
Salt and freshly ground pepper
6   mini brioche buns, split and toasted
Ketchup and pickle slices, for serving
Crispy Onion Rings (below)

Light a grill. Combine the chuck and short rib; season with salt and pepper. Form the meat into 6 patties. Grill over high heat, turning once, about 6 minutes for medium-rare. Set the burgers on the toasted buns, top with ketchup and pickles and serve with the onion rings.

CRISPY ONION RINGS Sift 3 cups all-purpose flour into a large bowl. Whisk in 1 cup water, then whisk in about 1½ cups seltzer, club soda or sparkling water until the batter is the consistency of very thick heavy cream. In a large, deep saucepan, heat 1 quart vegetable oil to 350°. Slice 2 large white onions crosswise into 1-inch-thick rings. Dip 8 to 10 onion rings in the batter to coat. Using chopsticks, lift out the onion rings, allowing the excess batter to drip back into the bowl, and add the rings to the hot oil. Fry, turning once, until the rings are deep golden and crisp, about 4 minutes. Drain on paper towels, sprinkle with kosher salt and serve. Repeat to make the remaining onion rings. Makes 6 servings.

SPANISH PORK BURGERS
"Gayane" plate by
Kenzo from Unica Home.

spanish pork burgers

FATHER'S OFFICE,
LOS ANGELES

Father's Office chef and owner Sang Yoon, who makes some of America's best burgers, flavors his succulent pork patty with Spanish ingredients like piquillo peppers and serrano ham. "Spain," he says, "performs miracles with pork."

4 SERVINGS

½ cup mayonnaise
1 large garlic clove, minced
¼ cup chopped flat-leaf parsley
1 tablespoon sherry vinegar
Kosher salt and freshly ground pepper
1 tablespoon extra-virgin olive oil, plus more for brushing
4 thin slices of serrano ham
2 pounds ground pork
1 tablespoon smoked paprika (pimentón de la Vera)
4 ounces Idiazábal cheese, shredded
4 crusty French rolls, split
4 whole jarred piquillo peppers, slit open

1. In a small bowl, combine the mayonnaise, garlic, parsley and vinegar. Season with salt and pepper.

2. In a skillet, heat the 1 tablespoon of oil. Add the ham; cook over moderately high heat, turning once, until crisp, 2 minutes. Drain on paper towels.

3. Light a grill. Mix the pork, paprika, 1 tablespoon salt and ½ teaspoon pepper. Shape into four ¾-inch-thick patties. Grill over moderately high heat for 5 minutes per side, or until just cooked through. Top with the cheese, cover and cook until melted. Transfer to a plate. Brush the cut side of the rolls with oil and grill. Spread the rolls with the mayonnaise, add the burgers and top with the piquillos and ham.

the guide

bar directory

Here's a listing of the restaurants, bars and lounges that created the incredible cocktails and bar snacks in this book. See page numbers below for the recipes.

ATLANTA

Ecco
P. 93
Charcuterie specialists
40 Seventh St.
404-347-9555

Holeman & Finch Public House
PP. 132, 187
Chefs' after-hours hangout
2277 Peachtree Rd.
404-948-1175

Restaurant Eugene
P. 175
Intimate bar and dining room
2277 Peachtree Rd.
404-355-0321

Trois
P. 98
Modish three-story brasserie and bar
1180 Peachtree St.
404-815-3337

BOSTON AREA

33 Restaurant & Lounge
P. 87
Back Bay hot spot
33 Stanhope St.
Boston
617-572-3311

The Beehive
P. 35
Boiler room turned jazz and cabaret club
541 Tremont St.
Boston
617-423-0069

Eastern Standard Kitchen & Drinks
PP. 35, 177, 189
Kenmore Square brasserie
528 Commonwealth Ave.
Boston
617-532-9100

Green Street
P. 74
Restaurant and bar with live jazz, Latin and world music
280 Green St.
Cambridge
617-876-1655

KO Prime
P. 164
Chic steak house
90 Tremont St.
Boston
617-772-0202

No. 9 Park
P. 159
French-Italian bastion
9 Park St.
Boston
617-742-9991

Rocca Kitchen & Bar
P. 186
Ligurian restaurant in a former South End warehouse
500 Harrison Ave.
Boston
617-451-5151

bar directory

BOULDER, CO

Centro Latin Kitchen & Refreshment Palace
P. 104
Lively cantina with a courtyard
950 Pearl St.
303-442-7771

Frasca Food & Wine
P. 149
Northern Italian dining destination
1738 Pearl St.
303-442-6966

West End Tavern
P. 142
Bourbon buffs' paradise
926 Pearl St.
303-444-3535

CHICAGO

Custom House
P. 154
Local-food-minded steak house
500 S. Dearborn St.
312-523-0200

De La Costa
P. 155
Euro-Latin club
465 E. Illinois St.
312-464-1700

The Drawing Room
P. 91
Subterranean lounge
937 N. Rush St.
312-255-0022

Encore Liquid Lounge
P. 95
Post-work, post-theater drinks spot
171 W. Randolph St.
312-338-3788

Le Bar
P. 147
Neo–Art Deco hotel bar
Sofitel Chicago
Water Tower
20 E. Chestnut St.
312-324-4000

MK The Restaurant
P. 80
Brilliant New American spot
868 N. Franklin St.
312-482-9179

Nacional 27
P. 171
Pan-Latin salsa and supper club
325 W. Huron St.
312-664-2727

The Violet Hour
PP. 72, 184
Cocktail connoisseurs' haunt
1520 N. Damen Ave.
773-252-1500

DALLAS

Aló
P. 138
Hip Mexican-Peruvian street food
4447 N. Central Expy.
Suite 100
214-520-9711

Fearing's
P. 193
Laid-back luxe hotel restaurant
The Ritz-Carlton, Dallas
2121 McKinney Ave.
214-922-4848

Shinsei
P. 156
Tex-Asian sushi scene
7713 Inwood Rd.
214-352-0005

Tillman's Roadhouse
P. 87
Rustically glam
restaurant and lounge
324 W. Seventh St.
214-942-0988

Trader Vic's
P. 174
Archetypal tiki-
themed bar
5330 E. Mockingbird Ln.
214-823-0600

HOUSTON

Backstreet Café
P. 177
1930s house
turned bistro
1103 S. Shepherd Dr.
713-521-2239

Benjy's
P. 134
Buzzing New American
dining room and lounge
2424 Dunstan Rd.
713-522-7602

Catalan Food & Wine
P. 197
Modern Spanish
dining room
5555 Washington Ave.
713-426-4260

Reef
P. 103
Jean-Georges alums'
kitchen
2600 Travis St.
713-526-8282

T'afia
P. 41
Locavores'
meeting place
3701 Travis St.
713-524-6922

LAS VEGAS

BOA Steakhouse
P. 67
Meat-eaters' mecca
The Forum Shops
at Caesars
3500 Las Vegas
Blvd. South
702-733-7373

Enoteca San Marco
P. 149
New Mario Batali
restaurant
The Venetian Resort-
Hotel-Casino
3355 Las Vegas
Blvd. South
702-677-3390

Fleur de Lys
P. 50
San Francisco star
chef's outpost
Mandalay Bay Resort
and Casino
3950 Las Vegas
Blvd. South
702-632-9400

Noir Bar
P. 130
VIP hangout
Luxor Hotel and Casino
3900 Las Vegas
Blvd. South
702-262-5257

Tao Beach
(seasonal)
P. 34
Rooftop poolside club
The Venetian Resort-
Hotel-Casino
3377 Las Vegas
Blvd. South
702-388-8588

bar directory

LOS ANGELES AREA

Craft
P. 59
Top Chef judge's
L.A. location
*10100 Constellation
Blvd.*
Los Angeles
310-279-4180

Crustacean
P. 58
Celeb-filled
Vietnamese spot
*9646 Little Santa
Monica Blvd.*
Beverly Hills
310-205-8990

The Edison
P. 77
Classic cocktail shrine
108 W. Second St.
Los Angeles
213-613-0000

Father's Office
P. 203
Hip tavern with
excellent food
1018 Montana Ave.
Santa Monica
310-393-2337

Ford's Filling Station
P. 84
Gastropub to the stars
9531 Culver Blvd.
Culver City
310-202-1470

Ketchup
P. 200
Glossy diner
8590 Sunset Blvd.
West Hollywood
310-289-8590

Kumo
P. 56
Japanese tapas
and sushi scene
8360 Melrose Ave.
West Hollywood
323-651-5866

Providence
P. 103
Seafood Shangri-la
5955 Melrose Ave.
Los Angeles
323-460-4170

Sona
P. 135
Neo-French restaurant
401 N. La Cienega Blvd.
Los Angeles
310-659-7708

LOUISVILLE, KY

Basa
P. 117
Modern Vietnamese
restaurant
2244 Frankfort Ave.
502-896-1016

**Maker's Mark Bourbon
House & Lounge**
P. 115
Bourbon authorities
446 S. Fourth St.
502-568-9009

The Oakroom
P. 114
Elegant dining room in
a century-old former
billiards hall
*The Seelbach Hilton
Louisville
500 Fourth St.
502-585-3200*

MADISON, WI

Cocoliquot
P. 174
French bistro and
wine bar
225 King St.
608-255-2626

**Fleming's Prime
Steakhouse & Wine Bar**
P. 52
Upscale chophouse
750 N. Midvale Blvd.
608-233-9500

Maduro
P. 57
Cigar and whiskey
devotees' hangout
117 E. Main St.
608-294-9371

Natt Spil
P. 114
Speakeasy-esque
after-party scene
211 King St.
No phone

MIAMI/FORT LAUDERDALE AREA

Cero Restaurant
P. 124
Health-minded sea grill
St. Regis Resort
*1 N. Fort Lauderdale
Beach Blvd.*
Fort Lauderdale
954-302-6460

DeVito South Beach
P. 104
Luxe Italian steak house
from *Wise Guys* star
150 Ocean Dr.
Miami Beach
305-531-0911

La Cofradia Restaurant
P. 80
Euro-Peruvian dining
160 Andalusia Ave.
Coral Gables
305-914-1300

Table 8
P. 48
L.A. hot spot's
Florida outpost
1458 Ocean Dr.
Miami Beach
305-695-4114

**Trina Restaurant
& Lounge**
P. 84
Oceanside restaurant
and lounge
*The Atlantic Resort
& Spa*
*601 N. Fort Lauderdale
Beach Blvd.*
Fort Lauderdale
954-567-8070

NEW JERSEY

The Boat House
P. 144
Cozy bar with
a nautical theme
8½ Coryell St.
Lambertville
609-397-2244

Circa
P. 39
European-style bistro
37 Main St.
High Bridge
908-638-5560

bar directory

Stage Left Restaurant
P. 75
Local favorite with an
old-school bar
5 Livingston Ave.
New Brunswick
732-828-4444

Verve
P. 71
Lively bar and bistro
18 E. Main St.
Somerville
908-707-8655

NEW ORLEANS

Arnaud's French 75 Bar
P. 135
Dapper, cigar-friendly
rendezvous
813 Rue Bienville
866-230-8895

**Café Adelaide & The
Swizzle Stick Bar**
P. 109
Playful homage to
1950s cocktail culture
Loews New Orleans
Hotel
300 Poydras St.
504-595-3305

Iris
P. 88
Up-and-coming chef's
New American
restaurant
8115 Jeannette St.
504-862-5848

Lüke
P. 148
New-fashioned
brasserie
333 St. Charles Ave.
504-378-2840

Napoleon House
P. 43
Venerable French
Quarter café and bar
500 Chartres St.
504-524-9752

NEW YORK CITY

Amalia
P. 124
Sprawling neo-baroque
drinking and dining
venue
204 W. 55th St.
Manhattan
212-245-1234

Bemelmans Bar
P. 160
Timeless New York
lounge
The Carlyle
35 E. 76th St.
Manhattan
212-744-1600

**Blue Ribbon Downing
Street Bar**
P. 183
Sliver of a bar serving
small plates
34 Downing St.
Manhattan
212-691-0404

Borough Food & Drink
P. 191
New York foodstuff–
focused dining room
12 E. 22nd St.
Manhattan
212-260-0103

Death & Co.
PP. 110, 163
Speakeasy-esque
boîte
433 E. Sixth St.
Manhattan
212-388-0882

Employees Only
P. 165
Bartender-owned
supper club
510 Hudson St.
Manhattan
212-242-3021

Fatty Crab
P. 66
Great Malaysian bar
snacks (and cocktails
by David Wondrich)
643 Hudson St.
Manhattan
212-352-3590

Flatbush Farm
P. 188
Hip comfort food
76 St. Marks Ave.
Brooklyn
718-622-3276

Flatiron Lounge
P. 38
Drink specialists
in an Art Deco bar
37 W. 19th St.
Manhattan
212-727-7741

The Good Fork
P. 123
Beloved Red Hook
restaurant
391 Van Brunt St.
Brooklyn
718-643-6636

Jack the Horse Tavern
P. 44
London pub–style bar
66 Hicks St.
Brooklyn
718-852-5084

Little Branch
P. 127
Subterranean
cocktail lounge
22 Seventh Ave. South
Manhattan
212-929-4360

Los Dados
P. 143
Cozy Mexican cantina
in the Meatpacking
District
73 Gansevoort St.
Manhattan
646-810-7290

Mercadito Cantina
P. 182
East Village taqueria
172 Avenue B
Manhattan
212-388-0162

PDT/Crif Dogs
PP. 34, 137, 198
Secret bar (PDT)
in a hot dog joint
(Crif Dogs)
113 St. Marks Pl.
Manhattan
212-614-0386 (PDT)
212-614-2728

bar directory

Pegu Club
P. 99
Encyclopedic cocktail
offerings
77 W. Houston St.
Manhattan
212-473-7348

Primehouse New York
P. 76
Stylish steak house
381 Park Ave. South
Manhattan
212-824-2600

Provence
P. 72
Elegant French bistro
38 MacDougal St.
Manhattan
212-475-7500

Public
P. 88
Designer-owned and
-appointed restaurant
210 Elizabeth St.
Manhattan
212-343-7011

Rayuela
P. 132
Pan-Latin restaurant
and lounge
165 Allen St.
Manhattan
212-253-8840

Resto
P. 192
Belgian gastropub
111 E. 29th St.
Manhattan
212-685-5585

Stand
P. 201
Burger dreamland
24 E. 12th St.
Manhattan
212-488-5900

Tailor
PP. 94, 108
Cocktail and dessert
destination
525 Broome St.
Manhattan
212-334-5182

Temple Bar
P. 39
Seductive cocktail den
332 Lafayette St.
Manhattan
212-925-4242

PHILADELPHIA

Amada
P. 118
Tapas tavern
217-219 Chestnut St.
215-625-2450

Chick's Cafe & Wine Bar
P. 68
Old-school watering
hole turned bistro
614 S. Seventh St.
215-625-3700

James
P. 85
Italian Market
neighborhood
newcomer
824 S. Eighth St.
215-629-4980

Tequila's Restaurant
P. 102
Exuberant Mexican
cantina
1602 Locust St.
215-546-0181

XIX Nineteen Café
P. 96
Refined dining in a
century-old rotunda
Park Hyatt Philadelphia
200 S. Broad St.
215-790-1919

PHOENIX AREA & TUCSON

Cowboy Ciao
P. 41
Italy meets the Old West
7133 E. Stetson Dr.
Scottsdale
480-946-3111

Ike's Coffee Bar & Cocktails
P. 49
Jet-setters' way station
Tucson International
Airport
7250 S. Tucson Blvd.
Concourses A and B
Tucson
520-573-8100

Jade Bar
P. 57
Desert lounge with sunset views
Sanctuary Camelback
Mountain Resort
and Spa
5700 E. McDonald Dr.
Paradise Valley
480-607-2301

Muze Lounge
P. 53
Hybrid drinking, dining and retail-clothing space
15680 N. Pima Rd.
Scottsdale
480-222-3366

PORTLAND, ME, AREA

Mims Brasserie
P. 151
French country–style comfort food
205 Commercial St.
Portland
207-347-7478

The White Heart Bar & Cocktail Lounge
P. 110
Downtown lounge with live music and DJs
551 Congress St.
Portland
207-828-1900

White Mountain Cider Co.
P. 95
New England farmhouse turned restaurant
Rte. 302
Glen, NH
603-383-9061

PORTLAND, OR, AREA

Andina
P. 158
Nuevo-Peruvian specialists
1314 NW Glisan St.
Portland
503-228-9535

Beaker & Flask
P. 62
Park Kitchen alum's new café and bar
720 SE Sandy Blvd.
Portland

Clyde Common
P. 166
Über cool hotel dining room
Ace Hotel Portland
1022 SW Stark St.
Portland
503-228-3333

El Vaquero
P. 81
Latin dining sensation
296 E. Fifth St.
Suite 221
Eugene
541-434-8272

bar directory

Paley's Place
P. 121
Local ingredients champions
1204 NW 21st Ave.
Portland
503-243-2403

Pok Pok
P. 194
Tiny Thai restaurant and lounge
3226 SE Division St.
Portland
503-232-1387

Roux
P. 151
A taste of New Orleans in the Northwest
1700 N. Killingsworth St.
Portland
503-285-1200

TearDrop Cocktail Lounge
P. 136
Cocktail craftsmen
1015 NW Everett St.
Portland
503-445-8109

RALEIGH/ DURHAM/ CHAPEL HILL, NC

Enoteca Vin
P. 59
Divine wine bar
410 Glenwood Ave.
Suite 350
Raleigh
919-834-3070

Humble Pie
P. 121
Cozy tapas stop
317 S. Harrington St.
Raleigh
919-829-9222

Lantern
P. 55
Lantern-lit Asian restaurant and lounge
423 W. Franklin St.
Chapel Hill
919-969-8846

Piedmont
P. 86
French-Italian bistro in a former warehouse
401 Foster St.
Durham
919-683-1213

South
P. 90
Elevated low-country menu
4351 The Circle at North Hills St.
Raleigh
919-789-0606

SAN DIEGO AREA

Blanca
P. 117
Sultry So-Cal dining room
437 S. Highway 101
Solana Beach
858-792-0072

George's at the Cove
PP. 36, 181
Newly renovated oceanside mainstay
1250 Prospect St.
La Jolla
858-454-4244

Modus Supper Club
P. 131
Urbane Banker's Hill
meeting place
2202 Fourth Ave.
San Diego
619-236-8516

Whisknladle
P. 106
Comfort-food fledgling
1044 Wall St.
La Jolla
858-551-7575

SAN FRANCISCO
AREA & SONOMA

**Absinthe Brasserie
& Bar**
PP. 146, 172
Belle Epoque–style
brasserie
398 Hayes St.
San Francisco
415-551-1590

The Alembic
P. 136
Newfangled pub
1725 Haight St.
San Francisco
415-666-0822

Bar Drake
P. 118
Lobby bar with a
master mixologist
Sir Francis Drake Hotel
450 Powell St.
San Francisco
415-392-7755

Bourbon & Branch
P. 75
Secret watering hole
501 Jones St.
San Francisco
415-673-1921

Cantina
PP. 77, 161
Latin-inspired cocktail
vanguardists
580 Sutter St.
San Francisco
415-398-0195

Cyrus
P. 78
Wine country
wonder chef
29 North St.
Healdsburg
707-433-3311

Elixir
P. 142
Cocktail savant in a
revamped 1800s
saloon
3200 16th St.
San Francisco
415-552-1633

Flora
P. 123
Upscale comfort food
in an Art Deco space
1900 Telegraph Ave.
Oakland
510-286-0100

Forbidden Island
P. 70
Kitschy tiki lounge
1304 Lincoln Ave.
Alameda
510-749-0332

Le Colonial
P. 44
1920s-style French-
Vietnamese throwback
20 Cosmo Pl.
San Francisco
415-931-3600

bar directory

Nopa
P. 45
Organic food luminary
560 Divisadero St.
San Francisco
415-864-8643

Orson
P. 107
New dining and drink
venue from Citizen
Cake chef
508 Fourth St.
San Francisco
415-777-1508

Poleng Lounge
P. 43
Pan-Asian dinner, dance
and DJ club
1751 Fulton St.
San Francisco
415-441-1751

Presidio Social Club
P. 199
Former barracks with
an officers' club vibe
563 Ruger St.
San Francisco
415-885-1888

Range
P. 91
Buzzing Mission
District restaurant
842 Valencia St.
San Francisco
415-282-8283

**Solstice Restaurant
& Lounge**
P. 40
Casual small-plates
space
2801 California St.
San Francisco
415-359-1222

Tres Agaves
P. 62
Transcendent
tequila list
130 Townsend St.
San Francisco
415-227-0500

SAN JOSE, CA,
AREA

Lion & Compass
P. 127
Silicon Valley stalwart
1023 N. Fair Oaks Ave.
Sunnyvale
408-745-1260

Martini Monkey
P. 63
Neo-tiki airport lounge
1661 Airport Blvd.
Terminal C
San Jose
408-925-9376

SEATTLE

Canlis
PP. 93, 170
Refined dining room
and lounge with a view
of Lake Union
2576 Aurora Ave. North
206-283-3313

The Great Nabob
P. 38
Cozy watering hole
819 Fifth Ave. North
206-281-9850

Vessel
P. 85, 122
Haute cocktail haunt
1312 Fifth Ave.
206-652-5222

Zig Zag Cafe
P. 131
Pike Place Market
refuge
1501 Western Ave.
Suite 202
206-625-1146

ST. LOUIS

Balaban's
P. 126
Old-school
American bistro
405 N. Euclid Ave.
314-361-8085

Monarch
P. 122
Acclaimed restaurant
and wine bar
7401 Manchester Rd.
314-644-3995

Pin-Up Bowl
P. 144
Martini lounge and
bowling alley
6191 Delmar Blvd.
314-727-5555

WASHINGTON, DC, AREA

Central Michel Richard
P. 138
Gastronome's
American bistro
1001 Pennsylvania
Ave. NW
Washington, DC
202-626-0015

Firefly
P. 115
Urban comfort food
1310 New Hampshire
Ave. NW
Washington, DC
202-861-1310

Proof
P. 148
Gallery Place
restaurant and
wine bar
775 G St. NW
Washington, DC
202-737-7663

Restaurant Eve
P. 60
Farm-driven menu
from a star chef
110 S. Pitt St.
Alexandria, VA
703-706-0450

liquor stores

Here's a list of top-shelf retailers—from boutique bourbon shops to liquor emporiums—that stock the spirits used to make the cocktails in this book.

BOSTON

Brix Wine Shop
This South End shop offers cocktail recipes and ingredient packages; there's a new Financial District outpost.
1284 Washington St.
617-542-2749
brixwineshop.com

STAMFORD, CT

BevMax
BevMax president Diego Loret de Mola is one of North America's top pisco experts.
835 E. Main St.
203-357-9151
bevmax.com

NEW YORK CITY

Astor Wines & Spirits
Known for its vast inventory, Astor opened a demo space in 2008 for cocktail seminars and tastings.
399 Lafayette St.
212-674-7500
astorwines.com

LeNell's
A compact Brooklyn store with an incredible array of bourbons and ryes, LeNell's sends out an excellent newsletter that includes a cocktail of the month.
416 Van Brunt St.
718-360-0838
lenells.com

ATLANTA

Mac's Midtown Liquor
In its large space, Mac's carries everything from micro-distilled gins to premium tequilas.
21 Peachtree Pl.
404-872-4897
macsbeerandwine.com

LOUISVILLE, KY

Liquor Barn
Master whiskey distillers conduct in-store tastings in each of six locations, including the flagship.
1850 S. Hurstbourne Pkwy.
502-491-0754
liquorbarn.com

NEW ORLEANS

Martin Wine Cellar
This NOLA institution has a broad range of spirits; the bourbon and Scotch selections are particularly strong.
3500 Magazine St.
504-899-7411
martinwine.com

HOUSTON

Spec's Liquor Warehouse
This 80,000-square-foot space carries some 40,000 labels of spirits, wine, beer and foods.
2410 Smith St.
713-526-8787
specsonline.com

CHICAGO

Binny's Beverage Depot
Besides selling exclusive spirits like single-cask Scotches, Binny's also helps plan parties.
3000 N. Clark St.
773-935-9400
binnys.com

Sam's Wines & Spirits

Sam's has four Chicago-area locations, including this Lincoln Park flagship. Their huge stock ranges from bitters to Bärenjäger.
1720 N. Marcey St.
312-664-4394
samswine.com

BOULDER, CO

Liquor Mart

Maintaining one of Colorado's best spirits inventories, Liquor Mart also sells big ice blocks for custom cubes.
1750 15th St.
303-449-3374
liquormart.com

LAS VEGAS AREA

Lee's Discount Liquor

Low prices are the draw here. Lee's Wine Club members get up to 50 percent off on selected spirits.
4427 E. Sunset Rd.
Henderson, NV
702-451-0100
leeswineclub.com

LOS ANGELES AREA

Hi-Time Wine Cellars

Family-owned for 50 years, Hi-Time specializes in rare old spirits like A.H. Hirsch 16-year reserve whiskey.
250 Ogle St.
Costa Mesa
800-331-3005
hitimewine.net

Wally's Wine & Spirits

Known for its wines, Wally's also has an excellent spirits selection, with more than 200 tequilas.
2107 Westwood Blvd.
Los Angeles
888-992-5597
wallywine.com

SAN FRANCISCO

John Walker & Co.

Opened in 1933 one week after Prohibition was repealed, John Walker specializes in hard-to-find brandies and liqueurs.
175 Sutter St.
415-986-2707
johnwalker.com

K&L Wine Merchants

A 30-year-old store (with two other California branches), K&L features great prices and a website that tracks inventory in real time.
638 Fourth St.
415-896-1734
klwines.com

SACRAMENTO, CA

Corti Brothers

This Italian specialty food store imports rare wines and spirits from around the world. Owner Darrel Corti buys casks of vintage Cognacs, which he bottles himself.
5810 Folsom Blvd.
916-736-3803
cortibros.biz

PORTLAND, OR

Uptown Liquor

Owner Russ Kelley is renowned for special-ordering unusual spirits for his customers, such as St-Germain.
1 NW 23rd Pl.
503-227-0338

recipe index

the guide
acknowledgments

Thank you. This collection of recipes would not have been possible without the help of these people.

Rebecca Anhert
Chris Beverly
Doug Bragg
Travis Christ
Robert Cooper
Rich Cruser
Bryan Dayton
Jill DeGroff
Marcovaldo Dionysos
Mike Donegan
Ben Dougherty
Lisa Laird Dunn
Damon Dyer
Will Earls
Ben Ford
Steve Fox
Michael Geist
John Gertsen
Justin Guthrie
Ted Haigh
Brian Haltinner
Ed Hamilton
Jenn Harvey
Mike Henderson
Robert Hess
Greg Hoitsma

Daniel Hyatt
Bertil Jean-Chronberg
Krista Johnson
Kristen Johnson
Ben Jones
Misty Kalkofen
John Knouff
William Kunderman
Francesco Lafranconi
Andrea Lazar
Don Lee
Julia Lisowski
Diego Loret de Mola
Brian Masterson
Ryan McGrale
Peter Meehan
Brian Miller
Daniel Moeri
David Mueth
Dustin Noel
Jean-Marc Nolant
Steve Olson
Nick Pandolfi
Christian Pappanicholas
Mark Pascal
Jackie Patterson

Edmund Pellino
Sasha Petraske
David Pickerell
Ray Pirkle
Christy Pope
Monica Pope
Kitty Puzon
Gary Regan
Francis Schott
Andy Seymour
Aisha Sharpe
Brian Shebairo
Willy Shine
Daniel Shoemaker
Valerie Simi
Jerry Slater
Eric Smith
LeNell Smothers
Andrea Spencer
Sefton Stallard
Amy Tingle
Ann Tuennerman
Neyah White
Rob Willey
Kareem Zarwi
Brian Zipin

More books from

FOOD & WINE

Best of the Best
The best recipes from the 25 best
cookbooks of the year

Annual Cookbook 2008
An entire year of recipes

Wine Guide 2008
The most up-to-date guide with more
than 1,000 recommendations

Available wherever books are sold,
or call 1-800-284-4145 or log on to
foodandwine.com.